KELTIE THOMAS

INSIDE HOCKEY!

ILLUSTRATIONS BY
JOHN KICKSEE

THE LEGENDS, FACTS, AND FEATS THAT MADE THE GAME

MAPLE
TREE
PRESS

Maple Tree Press Inc.
51 Front Street East, Suite 200, Toronto, Ontario M5E 1B3
www.mapletreepress.com

Distributed in Canada by Raincoast Books
9050 Shaughnessy Street,
Vancouver, British Columbia V6P 6E5

Distributed in the United States by
Publishers Group West
1700 Fourth Street
Berkeley, California 94710

Dedication
For my Dad whose stories of Rocket Richard introduced
me to the game

Acknowledgments
Many thanks to everyone at Maple Tree Press,
the Ontario Arts Council, John Kicksee, and Kix by Design

Cataloguing in Publication Data
Thomas, Keltie
   Inside hockey : the legends, facts, and feats that made the game /
Keltie Thomas ; illustrator, John Kicksee.

ISBN 978-1-897349-28-1 (bound).
ISBN 978-1-897349-29-8 (pbk.)

   1. Hockey—Juvenile literature. I. Kicksee, John II. Title.

Library of Congress Control Number: 2008925717

Design & art direction: Kix By Design
Illustrations: John Kicksee
Photo Credits: see page 63

We acknowledge the financial support of the Canada Council for the Arts, the Ontario
Arts Council, the Government of Canada through the Book Publishing Industry
Development Program (BPIDP), and the Government of Ontario through the Ontario
Media Development Corporation's Book Initiative for our publishing activities.

ONTARIO ARTS COUNCIL
CONSEIL DES ARTS DE L'ONTARIO

Printed in China

A   B   C   D   E   F

CONTENTS

ANYTHING CAN HAPPEN IN HOCKEY

Chances are you've heard that hockey is the fastest and coolest game on Earth. After all, it is played on ice and players zip around on skates covering 6 to 10 m (20 to 30 ft.) in a single second. But did you know that almost anything can happen in hockey? Oh, sure, the game has rules, all right. But that doesn't mean players always stick to them. What's more, sometimes players, coaches, and fans find sneaky ways of getting around the regulations. The fact is, when a bunch of people carrying sticks go out on the ice to battle for a black rubber puck, the action can get a little crazy and, well, downright unruly.

What other game do you know in which a player puked his guts out to deliver his best performance? Or a coach ordered the entire team to swarm a teammate for scoring? Or a player scored while skating backwards? Or a girl became one of the guys? Or the fans tried to melt the ice to stop the visiting team in their tracks? Sound too bizarre to be true?

You'll find all these true stories of the game and more in this book. Get set to enter the wild world of hockey where nobody knows what's going to happen next.

CHAPTER ONE

GOALS
ARE TO SHOOT FOR

Nothing can lift or sink a team's fortunes in the blink of an eye quite like a goal. Scoring goals is the object of hockey and the team who scores the most wins. You just can't win a game without goals. So teams fight it out for them, great players go get them, goal judges red-light them, fans jump out of their seats for them, and goalies downright despise them. Some goals are pretty, some goals are ugly, and some are just plain wacky. After all, it's a tough job to shoot a hunk of bouncing rubber past a goalie who covers most of the net, not only with his body but with some 22 kg (50 lbs) of gear all designed to stop shots. Nevertheless, top players have a knack of making scoring look oh-so-easy. Get the inside scoop on the greatest goal-scorers of all time and some of the strangest shots to ever cross the goal line.

FIND OUT
THE SCORE

HE SHOOTS HE SCORES!

Some players are like shooting stars. They streak across the ice and light up the rink—and the goal light—with their blazing shot. Check out some of the best goal scorers to ever fire up the game.

GORDIE HOWE

"MR. HOCKEY": Gordie Howe had it all—size, strength, good skating, a fighting spirit, and a quick hard shot. Maybe that's why he was known as Mr. Hockey.

SECRET WEAPON: Howe could shoot either way. "Go home. You'll never make it in the big league, kid." That's what the New York Rangers told Howe at their training camp in 1943. So the 15-year-old went back to Saskatoon, but he didn't stop playing. A year later, a scout invited Howe to try out for the Detroit Red Wings. Manager Jack Adams noticed that the big kid could shoot both right-handed and left-handed. He signed Howe on the spot. At first, Howe got so many penalties for fighting that Adams gave him a talking-to: "Look here, kid, nobody can score while he's in the penalty box. Stop trying to be the heavyweight champion of the National Hockey League and start being the scoring champion!" And that's exactly what Howe did. He won the scoring championship six times and finished 20 seasons straight as one of the top five scorers.

SCORING FEAT: When Howe retired from the NHL, he owned almost every scoring record there was. Then he came back to play for the World Hockey Association, becoming the only player to play over five decades. Howe got a record-setting 975 career goals.

MR. HOCKEY
9

BOBBY HULL

"THE GOLDEN JET": Hull flew around the rink at almost 50 km (31 miles) per hour. Thanks to his supersonic speed and mop of blond hair, sportswriters and fans called Hull "The Golden Jet."

SECRET WEAPON: A lethal slapshot. Goalies didn't wear masks when Bobby Hull entered the NHL in 1957. But some goalies say the speedy left-winger's slapshot drove them to it. Maybe that's because Hull's slapshot packed enough power to knock a goalie out. One time, his slapshot smacked Gump Worsley in the head. The goalie collapsed unconscious onto the ice and woke up in the hospital later with a worried Bobby Hull by his side. Experts decided to measure the speed of Hull's slapshot. The lethal scoring weapon clocked in at more than 189 km (118 miles) per hour—56 km (35 miles) per hour faster than the average player! They also found that his wrist shot streaked toward the net at 160 km (100 miles) per hour. Is it any wonder the Golden Jet took off as a top goal scorer, netting 729 career goals?

SCORING FEAT: In 1966, the Golden Jet broke the 50-goal barrier, with 54 goals. Till then no player had been able to score more than 50 goals in one season. A few years later Hull broke his own record by netting 58.

GUY LAFLEUR

"THE FLOWER": Fans called Lafleur by the English translation of his last name, for his artistic playmaking flair and beautiful goals.

SECRET WEAPON: The passion to make it happen. When he was 7 years old, Lafleur slept in his hockey equipment so he'd be ready to play first thing in the morning. The young hockey fanatic played morning, noon, and night. And this passion for the game never left him. When Lafleur played for the Montreal Canadiens in the 1970s, he'd be ready to go in his uniform and skates at 4 o'clock in the afternoon for an 8 o'clock evening game. Lafleur could pirouette circles around opponents as he carried the puck on the fly. He also had a deadly shot that he could put anywhere he chose. Lafleur became the go-to guy for the Canadiens. When Montreal was in the clutch, he'd zoom down the ice with the puck dancing on his stick and come up with a breathtaking goal.

SCORING FEAT: Lafleur became the first player in the league to rack up at least 50 goals and 100 points in six seasons straight.

Inside Scoop: Mike Bossy was a natural goal scorer. When the New York Islanders drafted him in 1977, he set a record scoring 53 goals in his rookie season. It was the first of a record-setting nine straight 50-goal seasons.

WAYNE GRETZKY

"THE GREAT ONE": No player has ever ruled the game or lit up the scoreboard quite like Wayne Gretzky. When he was a mere 10 years old, "the Great One" went on a scoring rampage that potted 378 goals.

SECRET WEAPON: Skating to where the puck is going to be. "Gretzky sees a picture out there that no one else sees," Harry Sinden, former General Manager of the Boston Bruins, once said. And he was right. Gretzky seemed to play the game with a sixth sense. He didn't skate to the puck. He skated to where the puck was going to be. This uncanny anticipation of how the play would unfold allowed Gretzky to outplay opponents, set up goals, and score goals in numbers never seen before. He also made plays never done before. For example, he'd take the puck behind the net then skate out either side and pass to a teammate, or flip the puck out front, or dart out front himself and heave the puck into the net on his backhand. He went to work so effectively behind the net that this area of the ice was known as "Gretzky's office."

SCORING FEAT: In 1989, Gretzky got his 1,851st point in the NHL, breaking Gordie Howe's record for career points. While Howe racked up 1,850 points in 1,767 games and 26 seasons, Gretzky smashed his record in just 780 games and 11 seasons.

"You'll always miss 100 percent of the shots you do not take."

— Wayne Gretzky on shooting the puck

THEY SAID It!

LEGEND ON ICE

The Rocket BLASTS OFF to Score

Maurice "ROCKET" Richard

Nobody could score like the Rocket. In 1945, Maurice "Rocket" Richard became the first player to score 50 goals in 50 games. In 1957, he became the first to score 500 regular season goals. Whenever his team, the Montreal Canadiens, needed a goal to get back in the game or clinch it, the Rocket alway seemed to come through.

"Sometimes he had a look on his face as if he were the only player on the ice," teammate Ray Getliffe said. "When I saw him coming towards me with that look, I wanted to jump over the boards to get out of his way. Can you imagine how the opposing team felt?" What's more, the Rocket had an explosive temper and often pounded opponents with his fists.

There was no holding him back. The Rocket could even score with an opposing player clinging to his back. No kidding! One time when Richard got a breakaway against the Chicago Blackhawks, defender Earl Seibert couldn't cut him off. So the big blueliner threw his arms on the Rocket's shoulders along with the rest of his bodyweight—about 95 kg (210 lbs). The Rocket kept right on skating, taking Seibert along for a ride. The goaltender moved out to block Richard. Somehow the Rocket managed not to buckle under Seibert's weight and to poke the puck between the goalie's legs to score.

"The Rocket kept right on skating, taking Seibert along for a ride."

THEY SAID It!

"When he's worked up, his eyes gleam like headlights.... Goalies have said he's like a motor car coming on you at night."

— Frank Selke, former Canadiens' general manager, on Maurice Richard

In 1952, the Rocket scored what may have been his greatest goal. The Canadiens faced the Boston Bruins in the seventh and deciding game of the Stanley Cup semi finals. The score was tied, 1 – 1, with four minutes to go. Richard had been knocked unconscious earlier when his head slammed into a Boston player's knee. Now he was stitched up and back on the bench. Richard still had blood on his face and was dizzy. Nevertheless, he went out on the ice, picked up the puck in the Canadiens' zone, and sped down the rink. He zipped around a Boston defender, and ripped the puck past the goalie. He may not have been completely conscious, but the Rocket could still score.

Inside Scoop: The Rocket streaked through the playoffs scoring a remarkable 82 goals. He racked up three or more goals a game not once but seven times!

Right wingers are usually right-handed shooters. They don't see as much of the net as the Rocket.

Did the Rocket have science on his side to score goals?

SCIENCE AT Play

Maybe. Usually a right winger has a right-handed shot. But not the Rocket. The feisty Canadiens forward shot left. So he carried the puck on his left, closer to the net than right wingers who shoot right. This gave the Rocket a bigger area of open net to shoot at than traditional right wingers.

A left-handed shooter on the right side will see more of the net, as the Rocket did.

WHAT A GOAL!

Every once in a while, a player pulls a crazy move on purpose or by accident unlike any seen or done before—and scores. Check out what can happen when players take a shot on the wild side.

Barging In on Net

She barges in on net and scores! The bold play bamboozled opponents and took everyone by surprise in 1894. Back then, two women's teams were going head to head at McGill University, when an inventive defense player turned on her jets to nab a loose puck. Instead of poking the puck down the ice and chasing it as players usually did in those days, she wedged the puck between her skateblades and sailed down the ice on her momentum. Once she ran out of speed, the player used her stick like a barge pole and pulled herself toward the net. Then she let the puck go and fired it past the goalie. The bizarre play netted her three goals before the game was even half over. Who knows how many more goals she could have barged in with if an opponent hadn't put an end to it by slashing her ankles?

Inside Scoop: Shame on you for scoring! In 1955, fans of the Montreal Canadiens booed Boom-Boom Geoffrion when he scored for the team. That's because the goal moved him ahead of fan-favorite Rocket Richard in the scoring race.

Henderson Takes Charge

The tension in the rink thickened as the last minute of the final game between Canada and Russia in the 1972 Summit series ticked away. The score was tied, so was the series. Each team was one goal away from winning—or losing—everything. A little-known Canadian forward, Paul Henderson, couldn't bear to sit on the bench any longer. Without realizing what he was doing, Henderson took charge. He ordered teammate Peter Mahovlich off the ice, leapt over the boards, and sped toward the Russian goal. Henderson fell down on the ice behind the net. He scrambled back up on his feet and got to the front of the net just in time to pick up a rebound from Phil Esposito's shot. Henderson fired away wildly, then got his own rebound and scored! The goal won Canada the series and went down in history as "the greatest goal of the century."

"I like it when my hands are sweaty and the crowd is yelling and one bounce can decide whether you win or lose something."
— Forward Ted Donato on being in the clutch

THEY SAID It!

He Falls! He Scores!

Fans don't call him "Alexander the Great" for nothing. Russian dynamo Alexander Ovechkin can score from the toughest of angles and even lying flat on his back. No joke! In 2006, Ovechkin scored a goal that became a legend overnight. He stormed over the Phoenix Coyotes' blue line, and Phoenix defender Paul Mara promptly knocked him down to the ice. But Ovechkin refused to give up. He thrust himself toward the puck as he rolled over the ice. Ovechkin slid on his back and, with just one hand on his stick, he drew the puck along the ice behind his head. Then he flicked the puck past the Coyotes' goalie Brian Boucher. Jaws dropped. Is it any wonder sportscasters hailed it as one of the greatest goals of all time?

Mario the Magnificent's Disappearing Trick

Mario Lemieux could play with the puck like a magician. His spellbinding moves often lured goalies to skate across the net. As they did, they would open up the five-hole between their legs and—presto!—Lemieux flipped the puck through the hole to score. One time, Mario the Magnificent's magical moves even made the puck disappear. As Lemieux sped out of his team's end, he tucked the puck between the skates of defender Ray Bourque, who was scurrying down the ice to defend his goal. Bourque had no idea the puck was there. When Bourque switched from skating forward to backward, Lemieux pulled the puck out of his skates just like pulling a rabbit out of a hat. The slick trick stunned Bourque and the goalie. Mario the Magnificent then zipped past the defender and slipped the puck into the net. How's that for a magic goal?

THE GAME WAS NEVER THE SAME

Boom! Zoom! In the 1950s, Bernie "Boom Boom" Geoffrion (left) drew his stick back up over his head, and slapped the puck. The Boomer's shot zipped through the air faster than any type of shot ever before. The slapshot was born and the game was never the same. Though few players used it at first and it's tough to shoot accurately with, today it booms off players' sticks all over the league (see Brett Hull, right).

STRANGE BUT TRUE

Cyclone Taylor Scores Skating Backwards

They saw him do it with their own eyes. Even so, many people couldn't quite believe it. Did Fred "Cyclone" Taylor really score a goal skating backwards?

Back in 1909, Taylor was at the top of the game. He had just led Ottawa to win the Stanley Cup and teams everywhere wanted to sign him. Taylor's phenomenal play drew sell-out crowds to the rink. Not only could he play any position, but he also had the speed and power to rush down the ice and stickhandle the puck past an entire team.

Taylor began his signature rushes by circling around his own net and roaring into his opponent's end. In his first game for Ottawa, he played defense and made five rushes up the ice with the puck that resulted in five goals. A reporter for an Ottawa newspaper dubbed him "Cyclone" and the nickname stuck.

When word got out that Cyclone had finally signed with Renfrew, Ottawa fans were devastated and sportswriters lit into him. Well, Cyclone shot back. He said he would "skate backwards and score a goal" against Ottawa. The fans and reporters couldn't wait to see it. In the first match between the two teams, Ottawa fans booed Cyclone's every move and he failed to score a goal on any of his rushes.

But the next time the teams met, Cyclone made good on his threat. He whirled up the ice, passed the puck to Lester Patrick, and twirled around to skate backwards. Cyclone then received a return pass and blasted it into the net.

"Wow! Did he really do that?" exclaimed spectators. It was a question people continued to ask Cyclone throughout his career. The strange thing was that he didn't say "yes" and he didn't say "no." But one time, Cyclone finally spilled the beans. "No, I never did score a goal while skating backwards. I know there are a lot of people who would swear they saw it happen, though," he said. And that was his last word on the subject. Just how Cyclone made it look as if he was skating with his back to the net, nobody knows.

CHAPTER TWO

GOALIES

ARE DIFFERENT

Goalies really are different than the other players on the ice. Night after night, the goalie stands in the line of fire as the lone guardian in net. Opponents pepper him with shots that can travel more than 160 km (100 miles) per hour. Yikes! A goalie constantly scrambles, falls down on the ice, and flings his legs, arms, and even his head to come between the puck and the net. In most games, stopping each and every shot is an impossible mission. What's most important is that the puck slips past a goalie fewer times than it gets by the goalie at the other end of the ice. Otherwise, the team loses the game. No wonder people say goalies are crazy. Meet some of the best and wackiest netminders of all time, and get the scoop on some unique equipment, plays, and strategies that they've come up with to tend the net.

STEP BETWEEN
THE PIPES

GOALIE GALLERY

Check out this gallery of goalies. Their rogue play between the pipes has inspired today's goaltenders and left a lasting mark on the game.

GEORGES VÉZINA

"THE CHICOUTIMI CUCUMBER": What do you call a goalie from Chicoutimi, Quebec, who remains as cool as a cucumber in the line of fire? "The Chicoutimi Cucumber," what else?!

SIGNATURE PLAY: Georges be nimble, Georges beat puck. When the Montreal Canadiens first laid eyes on Vézina in 1910, the local Chicoutimi goalie looked bored stiff and a little gangly. The young goaltender was leaning against a goalpost and said little. But once the Canadiens began pelting him with shots, Vézina stood up and jumped all over the puck. His amped-up, stand-up style stymied the Canadiens and was perfect for the era. For in those days, goalies weren't allowed to fall on the ice to make a save. The Canadiens couldn't get the puck by Vézina for a single goal! They were so blown away by his play that they signed him up.

MARK: The Vézina Trophy, awarded each year to the best NHL goalie, immortalized his name and "upstanding" play.

TERRY SAWCHUK

"UKIE": "The Uke was the best goalie I ever saw," sharpshooter Gordie Howe once said. Teammates called Terry Sawchuk "The Uke" or "Ukie" after his Ukrainian heritage.

SIGNATURE PLAY: The Sawchuk crouch. Back in the 1950s, the Uke was the first goalie to crouch between the pipes. Some people thought the strange stance made him look like a gorilla. But as Sawchuk said, "When I'm crouching low, I can keep better track of the puck through the player's legs on screen shots." The gorilla-like crouch also improved Sawchuk's speed and allowed him to kick out his legs quickly to stop shots. Soon young goalies everywhere began copying the Sawchuk crouch. Was it a case of monkey see, monkey do? Well, whatever it was, many people say Sawchuck is the best goaltender who ever played.

MARK: A record-setting 103 game shutouts.

THE GAME WAS NEVER THE SAME

Montreal Maroon goalie Clint Benedict wore the first mask in the game in 1930. But Benedict said it blocked his vision on low shots and soon took it off for good. It wasn't until 1959 that goaltender Jacques Plante (left) designed a facemask that didn't hamper a goalie's view. Soon after that, goalies wore masks game in and game out. Plante's design provided goalies with protection they'd never had before and helped them face the pressure of stopping the puck head-on. As former NHL goalie George Gardner once said, "Before we started wearing masks, I had nightmares before every game. I'd wake up in the middle of the night in a cold sweat. I'd see my teeth floating in a pool of blood."

JOHNNY BOWER

"THE CHINA WALL": Teammates called Johnny Bower "The China Wall," because he shut the puck out of the net as effectively as the Great Wall of China.

SIGNATURE PLAY: The poke check. Bower excelled at poking the puck away from shooters before they could shoot. The daring goalie, who backstopped the Toronto Maple Leafs during the 1960s, once said, "I practiced by lining up pucks in front of the net and diving out to poke them away." One time when Montreal Canadiens sniper Yvan Cournoyer zoomed in with the puck in double OT, Bower poke-checked the puck into the corner. A teammate fished it out and passed it to Bobby Pulford who scored, winning the game for the Leafs.

MARK: Playing in the minors for eight seasons before cracking the NHL and becoming a star.

DOMINIK HASEK

"THE DOMINATOR": Hasek's nickname aptly describes his amazing ability to dominate games with rock-solid focus.

SIGNATURE PLAY: Flopping around the net like a fish. Dominik Hasek has a style all his own. When he entered the NHL, people thought he looked so awkward that only luck kept the puck from slipping past him! Hasek drops onto the ice on almost every shot. He flops, sprawls, or twists around like a contortionist to cover the bottom of the net. What's more, he'll fling almost any part of his body—including his head—up or out to make a save. Then there's the Hasek roll. If he goes down stacking his pads to the right and a rebound goes to the left, for example, he rolls over on his back and stacks his pads to the left. The fact is, Hasek is extremely flexible. And this foils shooters because they never know what he'll do next!

MARK: Many people say that he's the world's best goalie.

Inside Scoop: In the 1920s, goaltender Howie Lockhart earned the nickname "Holes" for letting in lots of goals.

Jacques Plante

THE MAN BEHIND THE MASK

Sure, goalies are different. But Jacques Plante stuck out like no other. When he came into the NHL in the 1950s, goaltenders usually hung tight in the crease. Not Plante. Jake the Snake, as one sportswriter dubbed him, often slid out to pass the puck up to teammates. What's more, he went where no goalie had gone before—behind the net to corral the bouncing rubber.

Plante's frequent excursions gave fans a fright, raised an army of eyebrows, and led to some close calls. But Montreal Canadiens coach Dick Irvin didn't ask Plante to change his style. "That boy is not only adding excitement to the game by dashing out after the puck," Irvin said, "but I predict he'll revolutionize goaltending."

Irvin was right. As Plante backstopped the Canadiens to win the Stanley Cup five times straight, he picked up the coveted Vézina goaltending trophy five times in a row along the way. Pro teams soon realized that handling the puck outside the crease is an important skill for goalies to have.

Plante also changed the face of goaltending forever when he insisted on wearing a mask the night after Halloween in 1959. That night, New York Rangers forward Andy Bathgate let a shot fly that walloped Plante in the nose and made a deep cut. The ref stopped the game for Plante to get stitched up.

However, Jake the Snake refused to return without wearing the fiberglass mask he had designed and used in practice. Coach Toe Blake was loath to let Plante wear the mask, thinking it would block the goalie's vision like other face protectors of the day. But teams didn't have backup goalies back then. So Blake had no choice.

> "Jake the Snake refused to return without wearing the fiberglass mask he had designed."

Lined up with the puck.

Lined up between the shooter and the puck.

Plante returned in the mask and Montreal won the game. He kept on wearing the mask, and goalies everywhere soon followed suit.

Not much got by Plante. Not even the size of the net. One time, when Montreal was in Chicago, Plante noticed that the back of the net didn't touch his back in the usual place. Officials then measured the net and found it was a few inches shorter than regulation height. Another time, when Plante began playing for the Rangers, he noticed that the Rangers' net was higher than normal and insisted it be corrected. After all, he argued, how could he compete for the Vézina goaltending trophy if other goalies had a smaller net to guard?

Inside Scoop: He knits, he stitches! Jacques Plante knit his own wool hats and stitched embroidery. But coach Dick Irvin refused to let him wear the hats in games. So the crafty goalie began knitting undershirts to wear under his uniform!

SCIENCE AT Play

Unbelievable!

Plante robs Russian sharpshooters on not one but five breakaways. That was the word on the rink in 1965, when Jacques Plante came out of retirement to tend net for the Junior Canadiens. Russia's top guns had shot "holes" through their last three Canadian opponents. Plante didn't know what moves to expect from them, but he did know that a shooter's stick carrying the puck "sees" more of the net than the shooter. So instead of lining up his body with the shooter's body, Plante lined up his body halfway between the shooter's body and the puck. That way the shooter had less open net to shoot at on the near side of the net. And if the shooter suddenly decided to shoot at the far side, Plante could poke check the puck away. The ploy worked. Plante stoned the Russian shooters cold, and the Canadiens won, 2 — 1.

ARE GOALIES CRAZY?

"If you want to be a good goaltender, it helps to be a little crazy," goalie Gump Worsley once said. Worsley wasn't kidding. Check out some of the bizarre things goalies have done.

Cool Hand Puke

In the 1950s, Chicago Blackhawk fans nicknamed Glenn Hall "Mister Goalie," because he was so tough to beat. And players jokingly called Hall "Ghoulie," because his face got so drawn and tight before games. But maybe everyone should have called him "Cool Hand Puke." Not only did Hall have a catching hand as quick as lightning, he was also infamous for barfing before almost every game and sometimes in between periods. Legend has it that the Blackhawks kept a bucket at the bench just for Hall to lose his cookies in. Even though playing goal made him miserable, Hall played a record-setting 552 games straight over a seven-year stretch. No goalie has ever dreaded the game so much yet played so many games so well.

Gratoony the Loony

"There was nobody weirder than him," former teammate Rod Gilbert once said. Gratoony the Loony—a.k.a. Gilles Gratton—played piano to relax before games. Though he'd never had a piano lesson, he tinkled the ivories like a pro. The odd netminder believed he had lived several lives—one as a Spanish count. In fact, he often complained of an injury the Count had suffered in battle. When Gratoony the Loony played for the New York Rangers in the 1970s, his performance was also out of this world. One time when the team was fighting for a playoff spot, Gratton refused to play because "the stars weren't lined up." The team lost the game and didn't make the playoffs. Then there was his drop dead routine. Gratton would drop to the ice as if he'd been shot—and then ask what the fans thought of his performance. Loony or what?

Sleepless in Montreal

Lorne "Gump" Worsley was the team clown of the New York Rangers in the 1950s and 60s. The chubby little goalie with crewcut hair was always cracking jokes. Once, when asked what team gave him the most trouble, Gump quipped, "The Rangers." During his 10 seasons with the Rangers, they failed to make the playoffs six times. Shoddy defense and poor checking from forwards exposed him to as many as 70 shots a game. Worsley often thought that playing for the Montreal Canadiens instead would be "a piece of cake," because he'd only have to face 30 shots on a bad night. But when Gump got traded to the Canadiens, he discovered that the Canadiens had solid defense alright—but unlike the Rangers, they were expected to win. So the once happy-go-lucky goalie began losing sleep from the pressure of playing for a winning team.

Inside Scoop: Gary "Suitcase" Smith had a unique way of dealing with pressure. In between periods, the NHL goalie would strip off all his equipment and jump in the shower. How's that for washing away your troubles?

Roy Winks to Win

Cocky, competitive, and a little crazy: Patrick Roy was all three. The legendary goaltender, who won a record-setting 551 regular season games, once said, "Playing mind games with shooters has always been part of my game." Roy was notorious for baiting shooters by opening up holes like the five-hole between his legs and then closing them to stop the shot with a shock. That was his way of trying to psyche out shooters. And it wasn't the only way he got into opponents' heads. In overtime of game 4 of the 1993 Stanley Cup finals, the Los Angeles Kings were coming on strong against Roy's team, the Montreal Canadiens. Kings' forward Tomas Sandstrom swooped in on Roy with a close, hard shot, and Roy came up with a big stop. Then Roy made eye contact with Sandstrom and winked, as if to say, nothing's going to get by me, dude. The sheer confidence of the gesture made an unforgettable impression that people talk about to this day. And maybe Roy's crazy wink crushed the Kings. The Canadiens won the game and then promptly beat out the Kings for the right to hoist the Cup.

Girl Crashes Guys' Game

Ever since she played goal for her brothers in their backyard, Manon Rheaume has been crazy about hockey. When she was five, she played her first game with boys. She teetered on her skates and tripped over her pads. But she never looked back. Rheaume began dreaming of playing goal in the big leagues one day. And if anyone told her that was crazy, she didn't listen. She kept on playing with boys and sharpening her skills. When she was 20, a scout for the Tampa Bay Lightning sent team director Phil Esposito a videotape of her in action. Esposito took a look and said, "A little small for a goalie, but he moves well. He has good reflexes. We can invite him to camp." When the scout confessed Rheaume was a girl, Esposito didn't take back the invitation. People thought Rheaume was crazy to go the Lightning's training camp. But Rheaume took the chance, and her dream came true. In 1992, she played between the pipes for the Lightning in a pre-season game, becoming the first woman to play in the NHL. And the news media went crazy, tripping over each other to cover the story.

STRANGE BUT TRUE

Buzinski the "Puck-goes-in-ski"

When the red light flashes behind them to signal a goal, some goalies cringe, some bang their sticks on the ice in frustration, and some get fired up, becoming an impenetrable wall for the rest of the game. Not Steve Buzinski.

Buzinski's big break came in 1942, when many of the New York Rangers were off fighting the Second World War in Europe. The team desperately needed a goaltender. Manager Lester Patrick sent scouts to "comb every town in Canada." Days later, a scout wired the message: HAVE YOUR MAN. WILL REPORT NEXT WEEK. HIS NAME: STEVE BUZINSKI.

The next week, a skinny little fellow arrived at training camp. This couldn't be "the man," thought Coach Frank Boucher. The little guy barely stood head and shoulders above the boards. But he was "the Buzinski" the scout had sent and Boucher had no alternatives.

So into the net Buzinski went and the Rangers lost their season opener to the Maple Leafs, 7 – 2. Early in the next game, Buzinski let in another seven goals. The strange thing was he seemed to think nothing of it. When Detroit Red Wing Carl Liscombe let a shot go way wide of the net, Buzinski scrambled out of the crease and caught it. He casually tossed the puck into the corner for teammate Bryan Hextall. "Hex, it's like picking cherries off a tree," he said, as if he'd been catching all the shots coming at him all night.

A little later, Buzinski made a glove save. Then he tried to shadow box a Detroit player and lobbed the puck into the corner—the corner of the net. Buzinski had scored on himself! The Rangers dropped the game, 12 – 5, and Buzinski soon earned the nickname "the Puck goes in-ski."

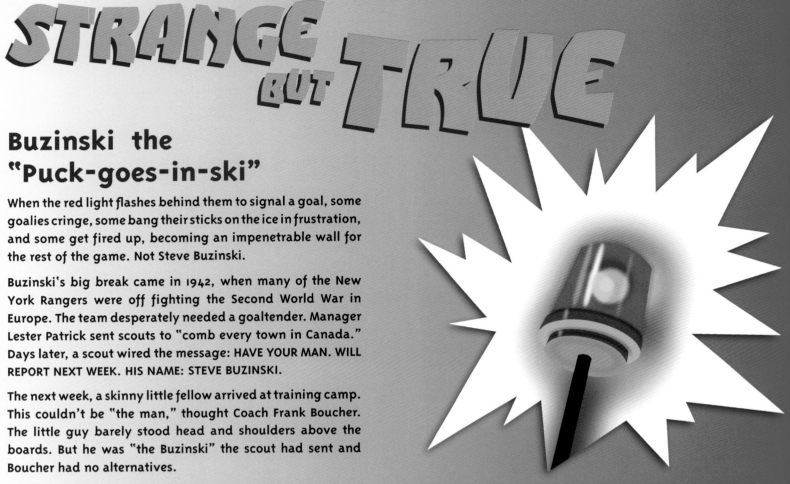

Nevertheless, the little goalie did provide comic relief. Once, Buzinski took a puck in the forehead and dropped to the ice like a corpse. The Rangers called for a penalty, claiming a Leaf's high stick had hit him. The Leafs argued it was the puck. Stick! Puck! Stick! Puck!, the teams shot back and forth. Then Buzinski sat up with a start, opened his eyes, and yelled "I got hit with the stick!" and promptly fell back onto the ice.

However, after nine games, Buzinski had let in a whopping 55 goals, and the Rangers were dead last in the league. The strange thing was that Buzinski didn't think he had played too badly. But his teammates didn't agree. They swore to quit until he was yanked out of the net for good.

CHAPTER THREE

JOKERS
ON DECK

Quick! Think fast: Why do most people play hockey? If you said, "because it's fun," you're absolutely right. Even pros play to have fun. In fact, some pros say that the key to dealing with the constant pressure to perform and win in big league hockey is to go out on the ice and have fun. And then there are some players who take having fun to a whole different level both on and off the ice. These players are the practical jokers and pranksters of the game. Almost every team has one and sometimes these jokers on deck can really get under their teammates' skin. What's more, if they get caught in the act, most feel no remorse. They just shrug their shoulders, or throw up their hands, saying "Hey, can't you take a joke? The laugh's on me, dude!" Get the scoop on some of the infamous pranks they've pulled and find out how their jokes can leave teammates in stitches in more ways than one.

HOCKEY JOKERS
ARE WILD

JUST JOKING AROUND

HA! HA! HA! HA! HA!

Sure, playing hockey is number one when it comes to having fun. But for some players, getting a laugh or a rise out of teammates is a close second. Just get a load of some of the practical jokes they've pulled to "bond" with the team.

Tricky Clarkie

Bobby Clarke—a.k.a Clarkie—was the heart and soul of the Philadelphia Flyers in the 1970s. The legendary captain, who led the Flyers to Stanley Cup victory, was known for hard work and true grit. Few people except his teammates knew what a prankster Clarkie could be off the ice. One time, when the team landed in Minnesota during a sub-zero cold snap, the Flyers suddenly noticed goalie Wayne Stephenson walking through the airport with one pant leg on and the other pant leg off. And what made the sight truly hilarious was that Stephenson didn't have a clue anything was amiss! Somehow, Clarkie had managed to cut off the pant leg without Stephenson realizing a thing. One of Clarke's favorite practical jokes was to drop his false teeth into the glass of an unsuspecting teammate. Now that bites!

KETCHUP

Hey Dude, Check Your Shoes!

One time when center Rob Niedermayer was on a road trip with his Junior team, he and his teammates hit a pizza parlor in Prince George, British Columbia. All of a sudden, partway through the meal, a loud ringing noise filled the restaurant. Niedermayer realized the sound was coming from a few teammates striking their glasses with spoons. Then he knew something was up. Tapping glasses was the team's prank alarm, signaling a "shoe check." It meant everybody on the team had to show their shoes. Niedermayer looked down at his shoes and discovered they were drenched in ketchup. He was so embarrassed! Some joker had doused both of them right under his nose.

HA! HA!

Stitches Bandit Strikes Again

Lindy Ruff's practical jokes often had his teammates in stitches. The defender, who played for the New York Rangers in the late 1980s, was a whiz with a needle and thread. No kidding! Ruff liked to sew teammates' pockets shut on the sly. When defender Randy Moller joined the Rangers, he became well acquainted with Ruff's tailor-made stunts the first time he suited up to practice with the team. As Moller stepped out on the ice, he tried to zip up his pants. But the zipper wouldn't budge. Talk about embarrassing! It wasn't long before the whole team noticed that the stitches bandit had struck again. Apparently, Ruff had turned Moller's pants inside out and sewed down the zipper so it wouldn't move.

OLD TIME HOCKEY

THE GAME WAS NEVER THE SAME

Gerry Cheevers (left) would do almost anything to get out of practicing. During one practice in the 1970s, the puck zinged the Boston Bruins' goalie in the mask above one eye. So Cheevers faked an injury and headed to the dressing room. But coach Harry Sinden didn't fall for the ruse and sent Cheevers back out on the ice. Trainer John Forristall decided to make a joke of it and painted 12 stitches on Cheevers' mask where the puck had struck. After that, Cheevers painted stitches on his mask wherever the puck hit it to show how many stitches he would have needed if he wasn't wearing it. Back then, all goalie masks were plain white. Cheevers was the first goalie to decorate his mask and he set a trend. Nowadays, masks painted with faces of scary characters, animals, or symbols (right) are standard goalie equipment.

THE JOKER'S FILES

Nick Fotiu

No practical joke was beyond the scope of Nick Fotiu. When the gritty left winger played for the New York Rangers in the 1980s, his teammates never knew what mischief he'd stir up next. The consummate prankster routinely substituted shaving cream for whipped cream on desserts, smeared black shoe polish on black phones, and "dusted up" teammates by sprinkling talcum powder into the dressing room hair dryers.

Fotiu loved a good laugh. When the Rangers were waiting for flights in airports, he often made them bust a gut with his money-with-strings-attached gag. Fotiu tied a $10 bill to a long string. Then he dropped the money on the floor and waited. The string blended in with the floor, so it was invisible. When an unsuspecting passerby tried to pick up the $10 bill, Fotiu yanked the string, pulling the money out of reach, much to the poor victim's embarrassment.

But usually Fotiu's teammates were the victims of his pranks. The crafty joker would do almost anything to get a rise out of them. When Fotiu found out that Phil Esposito hated bugs, for example, he began planting cockroaches in the star scorer's equipment. Esposito went ballistic when he went to put on his elbow pads or hockey pants and discovered a live roach crawling in them. And Fotiu? Well, he just cracked up.

But the roach capers were mild compared to Fotiu's lobster prank. Late one night during a road trip, Fotiu noticed a

" Fotiu swathed goalie John Davidson's truck in reams of toilet paper. "

lobster tank in the restaurant of the hotel where the team was staying. He snatched a lobster out of the tank and took it to his room. He removed the elastic bands on the lobster's claws then stuck the crustacean smack dab in the middle of the chest of his sleeping roommate, Bill Goldsworthy.

The lobster slid off. But Fotiu was undeterred. He picked it up and put it on Goldsworthy again. The creature began to crawl across Goldsworthy's chest and the poor player woke up with a start. Goldsworthy let out a scream loud enough to wake up the entire hotel.

Another night, Fotiu swathed goalie John Davidson's truck in reams of toilet paper. Davidson arrived at his truck just in time to see Fotiu making his getaway, waving and honking his car horn as he sped off. Later that night, Davidson and a few other Rangers decided it was payback time. They stole over to Fotiu's place and wrapped the house in toilet paper, along with all the trees in the yard. When they were done, the whole house looked white. Then they rang the doorbell and waited. Fotiu came out, and he was stunned. For the first time in his checkered joking career, he didn't laugh himself silly. He didn't guffaw, chuckle, or even let out a giggle. Fotiu called the cops to report a case of vandalism! His teammates laughed so hard they couldn't drag themselves away from the scene of the joke till the cops came.

"You've come a long way in two weeks, rookie."

— John Ferguson, General Manager of the New York Rangers, after waking up from an in-flight snooze and discovering that Nick Fotiu had covered his face in shaving cream and sprinkled nuts on top

THEY SAID It!

Inside Scoop: New York Rangers' fans adored Nick Fotiu for his fun-loving habit of lobbing pre-game practice pucks high up into the "cheap seats" where pucks never reach.

STRANGE BUT TRUE

You're Joking, Right?

You never know what's going to happen in hockey. That's what players, fans, and coaches all say. Well, on March 17, 1993, Esa Tikkanen, a pesky forward for the Edmonton Oilers, discovered just how true that is.

Back then "The Great One," Wayne Gretzky, had long been traded to the Los Angeles Kings. Edmonton general manager Glen Sather had also dealt away several other veterans who Tikkanen had won Stanley Cups with during the Oilers heyday—Mark Messier, Kevin Lowe, Jeff Beukaboom, and Adam Graves.

"Tik," as teammates affectionately called him, was adjusting to the new lineup. The Oilers were in New York to take on the Rangers at Madison Square Garden. Tikkanen did the morning skate with the Oilers, chowed down the pre-game meal with them, and then hit his hotel room to catch some afternoon zzzzzs.

Brrrrring! The phone rang in Tikkanen's room at 4:00 p.m. Oilers' public relations director Bille Tuele was on the line. He told Tik that assistant coach Teddy Green wanted to see him. Right away, Tikkanen knew Sather had traded him. "Where am I going?" he said.

Tuele stayed mum and told Tikkanen to talk to the assistant coach. Tikkanen jumped out of bed and tracked down Green. "You're going to New York," Green said. Well, there are a couple of teams in New York, Tik pointed out.

"The Rangers," said Green. "You play against us at the Garden tonight."

Tik was blown away. He'd be teammates with Messier, Lowe, Beukaboom, and Graves all over again! On the way back to his room, he bumped into Oiler pals Craig MacTavish and Kelly Buchberger. He gave them the news but, sure he was joking, they refused to believe him.

The three of them hailed a cab to Madison Square Garden and headed to the dressing rooms. The visitors' dressing room was on the right and the Rangers' was on the left. As MacTavish and Buchberger headed to the right, Tik went to the left. "See you later, guys," he waved.

But maybe the real joke was on Sather. The very next year Tikkanen and the rest of the ex-Oilers led the Rangers to their first Stanley Cup victory in 54 years.

CHAPTER FOUR

HOCKEY

HIJINKS

Mischief, mayhem, and monkey business. They sure do have a way of creeping onto the ice in hockey. Maybe that's because some players, coaches, and fans would do almost anything to win. Throughout hockey history, players have come up with inventive moves and sly "additions" to equipment that help them beat or stop the opposition cold. And when they're successful, their moves and equipment get copied by other players or outlawed by the rules of the game. So they're constantly on the lookout for new ways to get an edge. Hockey fans are also looking for ways to give their favorite team an edge. Sometimes fans even go so far as to take the game into their own hands. Get the scoop on the wild and wacky shenanigans of players, coaches, and devoted fans.

THE CROWD GOES WILD...

ON ICE SHENANIGANS

Whoa! Did you see what Sid the Kid did? Sometimes, players do the most peculiar things in games. Check out some of their infamous plays and questionable moves.

"Spider Web" Catches Puck

Before every game, Tony Esposito, the star Chicago Blackhawks goalie of the 1970s, paced back and forth, ranting that he hated hockey and wished he had another job. But as soon as he got between the pipes, Esposito didn't let a puck fly past him. Not only did he dive and scramble to stop shots, but he also designed and stitched improvements into his goaltending gear. Some of Esposito's improvements went over better than others. The trapper catching glove he invented, for example, made the glove almost twice as wide as it was before. It was an instant hit with both goalies and the league. Then there was the elastic mesh net that Esposito sewed between the legs of his goalie pants. Like a spider web, it was supposed to stop pucks from slipping through the five-hole. It did the trick alright. One time, a shot hit the web and bounced back at the shooter—almost nailing him in the face. The league was not impressed and soon outlawed that piece of gear.

THE GAME WAS NEVER THE SAME

In the 1920s, Fred "Cyclone" Taylor of the Vancouver Millionaires had a sure-fire way of clearing the puck. When the opposition came on strong in the Millionaire's end, Cyclone Taylor picked up the puck with his hands and tossed it into the stands! The play worked so well other players wasted no time copying it. But the NHL didn't share their enthusiasm. In 1928, the league outlawed the play with a rule that no player but the goalie can close his hand around the puck.

SCIENCE AT *Play*

Goalie Snows Sharp Shooter

On April 1, 1995, the Detroit Red Wings were leading the Dallas Stars 3 — 2. Less than a minute was left to go in the third period, when the ref called for a penalty shot against Detroit. As Red Wings' captain Steve Yzerman protested the call, goalie Chris Osgood surreptitiously prepared to stop the shot. Osgood scooped up some slushy snow around the goal and spread it over the ice in front of his crease. The ref didn't notice and when the Stars' Dave Gagner tried to deke Osgood on the penalty shot, the puck stayed glued to the spot in Osgood's "snowbank." Gagner looked like he had flubbed the shot and footage of the "blooper" aired on TV over and over.

Don Cherry Puts Crosby in the Doghouse

He hotdogs, he scores! That was story in 2003 when Sidney Crosby played for the junior team Rimouski Oceanic. Rimouski was shellacking the Quebec Remparts, 4 – 0. Crosby had already potted one goal and set up two others when he began vying for another from behind the net. He pressed his stick down on the puck and flipped the puck up onto his stick blade. Crosby held the stick steady at chest height and wrapped the stick around the net—and the goalie—to score. All the while Crosby held the puck flat on his stickblade. Unbelievable! The slick goal was captured on videotape. Don Cherry saw it and lambasted Crosby on Hockey Night in Canada, saying it was a hotdog move that the Remparts would remember the next time they played and Crosby would get hurt for it. Others disagreed, saying it was thrilling goal by a talented kid. And Crosby? Well, Sid the Kid said it was a move he'd practiced and he was so happy it worked in a game.

The Slash of '72

Emotions boiled over during the 1972 Summit Series between Canada and Russia. National pride was on the line and the Red Army took a commanding lead, demolishing Canada's top pros with superior skills and physical conditioning. But the Canadians fought back. In Game 6, Bobby Clarke (above right) whacked Soviet star Valeri Kharlamov's sore ankle, delivering a brutal two-handed slash. The slash injured Kharlamov (above left) and proved to be a turning point in the series, which Canada rallied to win. Afterwards, some people said it was a dirty play that had no place in the game. Others disagreed (see "They Said It," below). And the hot-blooded debate continues to this day.

SIDNEY

"I called Clarke over to the bench, looked over at Kharlamov and said, 'I think he needs a tap on the ankle'."
— Team Canada's assistant coach John Ferguson on the "slash of '72"

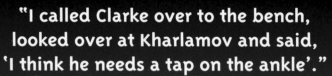

THEY SAID It!

FANS TAKE CHARGE

WE'RE #1

Everybody knows fans get charged up about the game. Check out some wild stunts pulled by hockey fans who decided to take things into their own hands.

SCIENCE AT Play

Hot Pennies Stick Fast

The hometown fans at Rhode Island Auditorium were fed up. The visiting team, the Pittsburgh Hornets, were sorely outplaying the Reds in a 1960s game for the Calder Cup. So the fans cooked up an ingenious way to stop the Hornets dead in their tracks. They heated pennies and threw them onto the ice. The hot metal melted the ice on contact and stuck fast, creating a skating hazard. Officials then had to stop the action to remove the pennies. Once the game got underway again, the fans hurled another barrage of hot coins. Officials begged them to stop. But the fans didn't let up until Pittsburgh Hornet "Wild Bill" Eznicki seized a fan's purse. Wild Bill proceeded to pry loose the pennies from the ice and dump them into the purse. Then he blew kisses to the fans and skated demurely back to the bench—with the purse in hand and no sign of giving it back.

Rocket's Punishment Starts Riot

Maurice "Rocket" Richard (see page 8) had a fiery temper almost as legendary as his goal-scoring touch. In 1955, the Rocket lost his temper during a game. He beat the stuffing out of Boston defender Hal Laycoe and gave a linesman a black eye. Clarence Campbell, head of the NHL, hit back. He suspended the Rocket for the last three season games—and the entire playoffs. Montreal Canadiens fans were absolutely incensed. At the next game, they pitched fruit and vegetables at Campbell and set off a tear-gas bomb. Then fans fled into the streets and launched a full-scale riot, breaking windows, looting stores, and overturning cars. In the end, the Rocket appeared on television and pleaded with fans to keep the peace.

GO TEAM GO!

Soccer Anthem Rocks Rink

All-star goalie Roberto Luongo makes no bones about his Italian heritage. Neither do his legion of 30-odd hardcore fans. When Luongo moved to Miami to play for the Florida Panthers, he found a "second family" at the Italian Pizza Time restaurant. Owners Bobby Cerbone and Guy D'Aiuto became fast fans of the young goalie along with lots of Pizza Time regulars. The fan club of sorts took to attending games and cheering Luongo with gusto. One time, the gang of fans broke into song, belting out the soccer anthem "Ole, Ole, Ole." The whole crowd joined in. Then the announcement, "Luongo's Legion is here" flashed up on the screen, giving the fan club a name.

Decked by a Handbag

Hack! Whack! Thwack! Players from both teams vie to get their sticks on the puck. Spurt! The puck squirts out of the scrum. A St. John's sharpshooter scoops it up and charges into the Twin Rivers' end on a breakaway. That was the scene in the Ottawa Valley League during the 1950s. And at least one Twin Rivers' fan found it too much to take sitting down. A little old lady sitting behind the boards hopped to her feet and whacked the St. John's shooter on the head with her big, black handbag. Ka pow! Ka thunk, thunk, thunk. The blow busted the handle, hurling the contents of the purse—three jars of cold cream—onto the ice and knocked out the unsuspecting shooter semi-cold. Just call it the curse of the purse!

"Send in the GAG line!"
— Rangers fans on the "Goal-A-Game" line of Rod Gilbert, Jean Ratelle, and Vic Hadfield, one of the highest-scoring lines in team history

THEY SAID It!

BEHIND the BENCH

It's not easy to be a coach. Not only do coaches have to prepare themselves for the game, but they also have to prep and motivate 20-odd players to all follow the same game plan. They must plot strategy, understand player psychology, and dare to try things everybody thinks are absolutely crazy. Check out some of their "finer" moments on the job.

New Coach Not in the Bag

Coach Roger Neilson had a reputation for wearing the craziest-looking ties and trying the quirkiest things to win. One time, when he was coaching a junior team, he got his dog Jacques to teach the players a "new" trick—fore-checking. Neilson let Jacques loose in front of the net and had players try to carry the puck out from behind the net as Jacques leapt toward them. But when Neilson found himself on the receiving end of crazy requests, he knew when to play it straight. In 1979, Harold Ballard, the cantankerous owner of the Toronto Maple Leafs, fired Neilson then rehired him just days later. The catch? Ballard claimed he wanted to keep the identity of the "new" coach secret until the last minute. So the belligerent owner asked Neilson to wear a paper bag over his head as he walked into the rink to the Leaf bench. Neilson flatly refused. He wore one of his crazy ties instead and took his place behind the bench to a rousing round of applause from fans.

THE GAME WAS NEVER THE SAME

Roger Neilson got nicknamed "Captain Video," because he was the first person to get the scoop on the competition by watching videotapes of their games. In the 1970s, Neilson spent hours analyzing game tapes of opposing teams to identify their weaknesses. By the 1980s, the coaching staff of every team in the NHL was doing the same. And video analysis changed the game. As soon as one team found a winning strategy, it soon spread around the league as other teams studied and copied it.

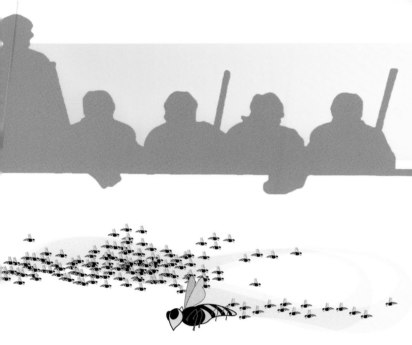

Coach Orders a Swarm

John Ferguson was as tough they come. When the rookie enforcer joined the Montreal Canadiens in the 1960s, he lost no time dropping his gloves, charging into the corners, and crashing the net. And he remained just as tough as the assistant coach of Team Canada in the 1972 Summit Series. With the score tied and only two-and-a-half minutes left to go in the seventh game, Ferguson and the whole Canadian bench held their breath as Paul Henderson got the puck. Henderson carried the puck through the entire Russian team and drilled it on net. The shot looked like a goal, but the goal light didn't come on. So tough guy Ferguson gave the officials a little "nudge." Borrowing a trick from his old coach Toe Blake, Ferguson ordered the entire team over the boards to swarm Henderson. That way, if the officials had any doubt about the goal, the players' celebratory antics might sway their minds. Whether the trick was needed or not, no one knows. But eventually the goal light came on.

Scotty's Uncanny Stick Sense

No one could "stickhandle" players like hockey's winningest coach Scotty Bowman (above). In the 1970s, Bowman coached the Montreal Canadiens to four straight Stanley Cup wins, and he was a stickler for curfew. Once, when the Canadiens trounced the Los Angeles Kings, Bowman gave them a midnight curfew. The team felt it was unfair, because they weren't playing the next night. Some players went out to celebrate anyway. When they arrived back at the hotel past midnight, the doorman held out a Canadiens' hockey stick and asked all of them to autograph it. The players obliged and the next morning Bowman fined every one of them for breaking the curfew. Did Bowman have a sixth sense for detecting curfew-breakers? No, but he did have a "stick sense." Bowman had given the hockey stick to the doorman, asking him to get the players who came in after midnight to sign it as irrefutable evidence.

Inside Scoop: Russian coach Anatoly Tarasov insisted star goalie Vladislav Tretiak toss and catch a tennis ball everywhere he went. Tarasov even had special pockets sewn into Tretiak's swimsuit to hold tennis balls at the beach!

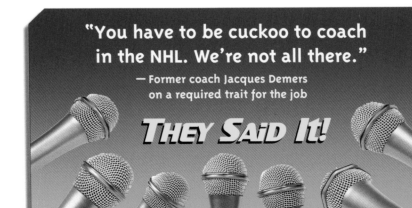

"You have to be cuckoo to coach in the NHL. We're not all there."
— Former coach Jacques Demers on a required trait for the job

THEY SAID IT!

STRANGE BUT TRUE

Sidney Crosby's Sweater Disappears

In January 2005, Sidney Crosby was on top of the world. The young star and his Canadian teammates had thrashed the Russians 6 — 1 to win the World Junior Cup. They packed their hockey bags, celebrated, and Crosby flew to Mont-Joli, Quebec, to rejoin his regular team.

But when he unzipped his hockey bag, his sweater was missing. The red number 9 sweater he had worn in the final game was gone! Crosby struggled to hold back tears. He had wanted to keep the jersey as a memento of the thrilling victory. And he was certain he had packed it in his bag. How could it have disappeared?

Hockey Canada filed a "missing sweater report" with police, the airline launched an investigation, and news headlines broke the story everywhere. If the missing sweater had been stolen, any thief would have a tough time wearing it or selling it without escaping notice. Four days later, a mailman found a red number 9 sweater, with a related news story clipped to it, inside a mailbox. The mailman was sure it was Crosby's. So was Crosby when he heard the sweater really stunk!

The thief soon confessed. Baggage handler Jacques Lamoureux had seen something red poking out of a hockey bag. When he discovered it was a Team Canada jersey, he took it. "I just lost my mind," Lamoureux told reporters. It was the very thing his 14-year-old daughter, a hockey player herself, had wanted for Christmas. The strange thing was, even as Lamoureux stuffed the sweater under his jacket, he knew stealing was wrong. So eventually he turned himself in. "I really enjoyed seeing Sidney Crosby smiling with his jersey on television after he got it back," said Lamoureux. "Maybe I was too much of a fan."

CHAPTER FIVE

REAL
SUPERSTITIONS

Can you imagine throwing away your stick if someone lays a finger on it? Or refusing to go out on the ice without your lucky undershirt on? Or talking to the goalposts as if they were your friends? Superstitions like these may sound silly or even crazy. Nevertheless, they're a tried-and-true part of good ol' hockey tradition. In fact, some players even believe they mean all the difference between playing a good game and a bad one. Get the scoop on players' superstitions and some of the strangest good luck charms the game has ever seen.

Good Luck!
Bad Luck?

**CROSS YOUR FINGERS
TO READ ON**

SUPERSTITIONS 'R' US

Check out some superstitions that hockey players use to rock and roll the game.

Gretzky's Sweater Tuck

Was the Great One superstitious? Maybe so. Wayne Gretzky liked to hide his hockey sticks in a corner so they wouldn't touch other sticks or cross one another. What's more, Gretzky always played with part of his sweater tucked inside his hockey pants. The ritual began when Gretzky was six years old. Gretzky was playing on a team of 10-year-olds. The team sweater was so big for him, it fell to his knees and kept getting caught on his stick. So his dad tucked the right side of it into his hockey pants. Maybe Gretzky thought it brought him luck, because he continued to wear his sweater like that until he hung up his skates for good.

The King of Superstition

No player has ever been more superstitious than Phil Esposito. When the high-scoring center got ready for a game in the 1970s, he first winked at a red horn given to him by his grandmother to ward off "the evil eye." Then he dressed right to left, pulling his right sock on first then his left, and so on. He had a teammate fix his shoulder pads, he pinned a "lucky" medal on his suspenders, and he placed his hockey stick on the floor between his legs so the blade pointed northwest. After that, Esposito had a trainer sprinkle white powder on the blade. And he didn't stop there. Then he'd look around the dressing room for any "unlucky" signs like crossed hockey sticks, and yell if he spotted one. Esposito also insisted that the team go out onto the ice the same way every game. One time, when he had a cold, he wore a black turtleneck to keep his neck warm and he scored three goals in the game. After that, the turtleneck became a good luck charm Esposito never played without.

Inside Scoop: Phil Esposito had an uncommon knack for scoring goals. Not only did he win the NHL scoring championship five times, but he also scored his 50th goal of the season on his birthday three times.

The Stick Nitpick

Jeremy Roenick knows that if you have a routine that works, you have to "stick with it." Before a game, the outspoken forward always eats pasta, drinks five cups of coffee, dresses from right to left, and chews two pieces of gum during the warmup. That's not all. Roenick never lets anyone—or even any other sticks—touch his sticks. If someone accidentally touches one of his sticks, Roenick throws it out or gives it away. What's more, he won't touch any other sticks. You might say Roenick is a royal nitpick for sticks!

SCIENCE AT Play

Are players' superstitions bunk?

Maybe not. Some research shows that superstitious rituals, such as eating special foods, dressing in a certain order, and wearing special clothes, may help players deal with mental stress before games. And if players can deal with this stress, they may play better.

ARE YOU TALKING TO ME?

Goalie Talks to Goalposts

Life between the pipes can be lonely. But not for Patrick Roy. "I talk to my goalposts," the stellar goalie once confessed. "It's a superstition." But that doesn't mean it was just idle chitchat. According to Roy, superstitions like this helped him concentrate. Before the opening faceoff of a game, Roy always skated out of his net to the blueline. Then he turned around and stared down the net. The longer he glowered at the net, the tinier it looked to him. This boosted his confidence. Then he'd have a chat with the goalposts. "They're my friends. They listen," he'd explain. Roy also talked to his goalposts during games by rapping them with his stick. And get this: Roy said the goalposts talked back with a "Bang!"

> "Other players have superstitions but we goalies call them habits."
>
> —Former goalie Glenn Healy
> on what makes goalies different

THEY SAID It!

LUCKY CHARMS

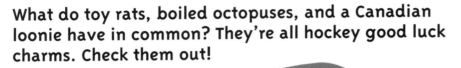

What do toy rats, boiled octopuses, and a Canadian loonie have in common? They're all hockey good luck charms. Check them out!

Eight Arms of Charm

What's slimy, rubbery, and purple and red all over? A boiled octopus in Detroit, of course. Two Detroit Red Wings fans cooked up this strange good luck charm in 1952. Brothers Jerry and Pete Cusimano, who ran a fish store, got excited about the Red Wings' playoff chances. "If the Wings win eight straight games, they'll win the Cup," said Jerry. Then inspiration struck him. "An octopus has eight legs. Let's take it to the game and throw it on the ice. It'll be good luck." And that's exactly what the Cusimano brothers did. They boiled up an octopus, turning its rubbery body from gray to purply red. Then they wrapped it in brown paper, smuggled it into the rink, and pitched it onto the ice. The ref skated over to the bright rubbery blob and jumped away as soon as he realized what it was. But the Red Wings' players didn't seem to recoil at all. They won the Cup in eight straight games. And the Detroit tradition of throwing octopuses on the ice for luck during the playoffs was born. Today, a giant fake purple octopus comes down from the rafters at Detroit to give the team eight helping hands before their games.

Inside Scoop: One time, Detroit fans heaved a massive 25 kg (50 lb.) octopus onto the ice. The crowd "oohed" and "aahed" as it made a mighty splat, and the ice maintenance crew took it for a ride on the hood of the Zamboni.

"You ever smelled a half-boiled octopus? It ain't exactly Chanel No. 5, you know."

— Pete Cusimano, one of Detroit's original Octopus Pitchers, on what makes an octopus a lucky charm that gets noticed

THEY SAID IT!

When the Rats Came to Town

Just before the home opener of the Florida Panthers' 1995–96 season, a rat bolted across their dressing room floor. Forward Scott Mellanby grabbed his stick and slapped the rodent as if it were a puck. Then, with a few rat hairs clinging to his stick, Mellanby went out and scored two goals in a 4 – 3 win over the Calgary Flames. "It wasn't a hat trick, it was a rat trick," quipped the Panthers' goalie John Vanbiesbrouck. The next time Mellanby scored, a fan threw a plastic toy rat on the ice. And after that, every time the Panthers scored, fans tossed tons of plastic rats onto the ice. One time, the rats rained down so heavily that a line official took cover in one of the nets! Games were delayed as arena staff scurried to clear away the rodents. But nothing could stop the downpour of rats. And the little rodents seemed to bring the team luck. That year, the Panthers made it all the way to the Stanley Cup finals for the very first time. The season went down in club history as the Year of the Rat.

Canuck Luck Is a Loonie

In 2002, Trent Evans secretly buried a loonie at center ice at the Salt Lake City Olympic games. The icemaker used the Canadian $1 coin to make a dot, because the circle where the referee drops the puck was missing. But Evans was also a proud Canadian, and he wanted to bring Canada's men and women good luck in the hockey tournament. In fact, Evans went so far as to tell the teams that they had a lucky loonie hidden in the ice. And the secret coin proved its mettle like no other lucky charm in the history of hockey. The Canadian women's team went on to beat out the US for the gold medal. After the game, Canadian forward Danielle Goyette kissed center ice to thank the loonie for its help. But teammate Hayley Wickenheiser rushed over and shooed away Goyette, so she wouldn't give away the secret coin before the men's final game. The Canadian men then fought their way to victory, winning Olympic gold for the first time in 50 years. And that's when Wayne Gretzky, general manager of Team Canada, got a mischievous twinkle in his eye, and revealed the secret lucky charm for the world to see.

THE GAME WAS NEVER THE SAME

The NHL was not thrilled by the deluge of rats Florida Panthers' fans tossed on the ice. At the start of the 1996–97 season, league bigwigs made "the rat rule." According to the new rule, if any objects were thrown on the ice, the home team could be charged with a two-minute delay of game penalty. Of course, there was nothing to stop fans from throwing rats on the ice after the game....

Coach Whips Up
Towel Power

"This refereeing is so foul, it's time to throw in the towel!" That's what Vancouver Canuck coach Roger Neilson must have thought during the playoffs in 1982. The Canucks were down 3 – 1 to the Chicago Blackhawks. Referee Bob Myers had called a string of penalties against the Canucks. Then Myers disallowed a Vancouver goal to send another Canuck to the penalty box. Chicago scored on the power play that resulted, and Neilson gave the ref a signal of his thoughts.

The Canuck coach threw a white towel on the end of a hockey stick and hoisted the makeshift "white flag" in the air as a mock gesture of surrender. Several Canucks on the bench did the same and the referee ejected Neilson from the game.

And the strange thing was that the white towel—Neilson's bogus token of surrender—turned into a symbol of power overnight. When the Canucks flew back to Vancouver for the next game against the Blackhawks, a fire truck escorted their plane off the runway. And it wasn't just any old fire truck. The firefighters had stuck hockey sticks with white towels tied to the ends in its fenders.

"Towel Power" then swept Vancouver fans off their feet and right out of their seats. During the next game, thousands of Canuck fans waved white towels in the stands. No one had seen anything like it. Vancouver won the game 4 – 3 and the flurry of white towels continued to rage throughout the rest of the playoffs, propelling the Canucks to the Stanley Cup

final. Though they eventually lost the Cup to the New York Islanders, Towel Power still rules the Canuck's rink to this day. What's more, sports fans all over North America wring out the power of the towel for their teams.

CHAPTER SIX

THE QUEST
FOR THE CUP

Why are hockey players so obsessed with winning the Stanley Cup? Maybe the Great One, Wayne Gretzky, said it best: "There's no feeling like lifting that Stanley Cup. It's the greatest thrill in the world." In the early 1890s, Lord Stanley of Preston, the Governor General of Canada, developed a passion for hockey. He donated the now-famous silver bowl as a challenge cup to be won by amateur hockey champions each year. (In 1926, the Stanley Cup competition became part of the NHL.) Ever since then, players—big and small, young and old—have all had the same dream: to win the Stanley Cup. Get the scoop on what it takes to win the Cup and some of the wackiest things winners have done with Stanley.

WE'RE HUNTING FOR
STANLEY!

CRAZY CUP CAPERS

Sure, players revere the Stanley Cup with infinite pride and awe. But once winners get their hands on the trophy, there's no telling what they might do to it. Check out some of the craziest Cup capers of all time.

Champions Get Their Kicks

Drop! Whomp! Whewwwww! That was the scene at the Rideau Canal one night in Ottawa in 1905. The Ottawa Silver Seven had just won the Stanley Cup, and they were out on the town whooping it up. Back then, the Cup was a silver bowl small enough for a player to tuck under one arm like a football. One of the Silver Seven carried it to a local hotel where the team celebrated into the wee hours of the morning. As the Silver Seven walked home along the Rideau Canal, star Harvey Pulford wondered aloud how far he could drop-kick the Cup up the canal. His teammates dared him to find out. So Pulford dropped the Cup from a bridge and kicked it high into the pitch-black sky. The Cup sailed through the air until it landed on the frozen canal with a clunk. Just call the incident a "kick-and-run," because the players left the scene without retrieving the Cup and stumbled home to bed. The next morning team officials came asking after the Cup to engrave it. Coach Alf Smith remembered the previous night's hijinks and hightailed it back to the canal. Luckily, the Cup was still there waiting for him to pick up. But it wasn't long before the Cup went missing in action again....

Inside Scoop: Bryan Trottier, captain of the New York Islanders, won the Stanley Cup four times in the 1980s. Legend has it that Trottier slept with the trophy one night.

Lafleur Kidnaps the Cup

In 1979, Guy Lafleur could do no wrong. Montreal fans adored the star forward whose singular scoring touch had helped the Canadiens rack up four Stanley Cup victories in a row. After the fourth win, Lafleur was itching to take the Cup for a ride. Back then individual players didn't get to hang out with Stanley for a day like they do today. So Lafleur concocted a plan to kidnap Stanley. He knew that Claude Mouton, the VP of Public Relations for the Canadiens, was safeguarding the Cup in the trunk of his car. So Lafleur made copies of Mouton's car keys, removed Stanley from the trunk, and spirited the Cup to his hometown, Thurso, Quebec. Lafleur's parents, friends, and neighbors couldn't believe it when he unveiled the Cup on his parents' front lawn. People touched it, kissed it, and hugged it. But later when Lafleur noticed his son watering the Cup with a garden hose, he decided it was time to return Stanley. And it was none too soon, because Mouton had already figured out the identity of the "Cupnapper."

Winners' Inner Circle

Not all Stanley Cup winners are content to have their name engraved on the outside of the Cup. Phil Bourque, the legendary Cup dunker who won the championship with the Pittsburgh Penguins in 1992 (see right), engraved his name inside the Cup, too. That summer, when it was time for Bourque to have his day with the Cup, he heard something rattling inside the trophy. So he took the Cup apart with a screwdriver and discovered a loose nut holding the bowl at the top. As Bourque tightened the nut, he noticed that the names of people who had repaired the Cup were engraved inside it. Compelled by a sudden urge to add his name to the list, Bourque inscribed it with the screwdriver—a feat that took three hours to complete. Satisfied with his secret handiwork, he promptly forgot about it until 1993, when J.J. Daigneault, who won the Cup with the Montreal Canadiens that year, said, "I saw what you did." Bourque was completely flummoxed: "How did you see it?" Daigneault broke into a smile, "Because, I put my name there, too."

Phil was Here

Stanley Takes a Plunge

When the Pittsburgh Penguins won the Stanley Cup for the second time straight in 1992, team captain Mario Lemieux threw a party at his home to celebrate. In the garden, Lemieux had a pool with a tall waterfall that sloped down to the deck. Goaltender Tom Barasso scaled the slope and took the Cup to the top of the waterfall. Around three in the morning, Phil Bourque, a gritty defensive forward, decided that Stanley needed to go for a swim. Wearing only his underwear, Bourque climbed to the top of the waterfall, heaved Stanley over his head, and pitched the Cup into the pool below. Splash! The Cup hit the water like a cannonball and sank to the bottom of the pool. The water in it made it so heavy that five or more players had to dive in and pull it out. The players took lots of pictures and the Cup slid back into the pool for the rest of the party. The Penguins kept the incident hush-hush because they didn't want to get into trouble. But they soon learned that it wasn't the first time Stanley had gone swimming. In fact, the keepers of the Cup at the Hockey Hall of Fame can tell how long Stanley has been hanging out in the pool just by looking at the Cup.

Inside Scoop: The silver bowl on top of the Stanley Cup trophy is a fake. In the 1960s, after the bowl had been drop-kicked, filled with copious bottles of champagne, and used as a flowerpot, hockey officials were concerned that it was becoming old and weak. So they had a replica made and put the real bowl under glass in the Hockey Hall of Fame for safekeeping.

LEGEND ON ICE

THE MOOSE TAKES MANHATTAN

Mark Messier

Teammates called Mark Messier "The Moose," because he was big, strong, and fiercely determined. Armed with a powerful shot, Messier had a mean streak and, as he matured as a player, he developed into a fearless leader, too.

When the Moose hit Manhattan to join the New York Rangers in 1991, "the curse" was the talk of the town. The team hadn't won the Stanley Cup since 1940. Their winless spell had lasted so long that many people were convinced the team was jinxed.

But Messier didn't believe in the curse. Maybe that's why the Rangers and their fans hailed him as their last hope of winning the Cup. The superstar center had led the Edmonton Oilers to five Stanley Cup wins—four in the team's glory days with Wayne Gretzky, and one after Gretzky had been traded to Los Angeles. And now the Moose was hungry for another.

The Rangers made Messier team captain and his all-out play inspired his teammates to try to match his intensity. In 1994, the Rangers made it to the Eastern Conference finals. Even though they had beaten their opponents, the New Jersey Devils, all year, the Devils took a 3 – 2 lead in the series. The Rangers were on the brink of elimination once again. But the Moose didn't blink.

"We know we're going to go in and win Game 6 and bring it back for Game 7," guaranteed Messier. Messier's guarantee made headlines everywhere and grabbed people's attention. "How can he be so cocky, so sure?" people wondered. "What about the curse?"

In Game 6, the New Jersey fans chanted "1940" relentlessly to remind the Rangers just how long it had been since they had won the Cup. Maybe the heckling worked. In the first period, the Devils grabbed the lead 2 – 0.

But toward the end of the second period, Messier dropped a pass back to Alexei Kovalev and Kovalev scored. The goal brought the Rangers back to life. Now they were down only one goal. When Messier came out on the ice for the third period, he had a look of pure determination on his face. He went on a tear and scored a hat trick. The Rangers won the game and the series and went on to play the Vancouver Canucks for the Stanley Cup. The final series went seven games until Messier scored the Cup-winning goal. Finally, the curse was broken!

THE NEW YORK NEWS

TODAY'S WEATHER

VOL. 11 NUMBER 11

NEW YORK, NY. THURSDAY, MAY 26, 1994

$ 0.75

"Mess" Guarantees Win Against the Devils!

"We know we have to win it," the Rangers captain said before last night's game. "We can win it. And we are going to win it."

"You look at his eyes, you think there's a screw loose."
— Hockey commentator Don Cherry on how the young Mark Messier played the game with reckless abandon

"He's the best clutch player... when the chips are down and there's a big game to be won, there is nobody better."
— New Jersey Devils' forward Bernie Nicholls on Mark Messier, his checking assignment in the 1994 playoffs

THEY SAiD It!

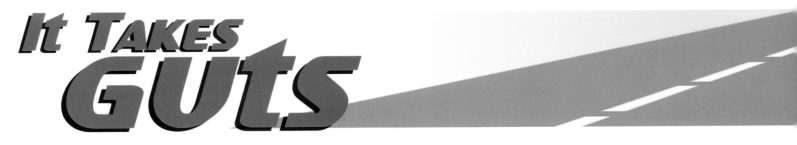

It Takes GUts

The road to the Stanley Cup is long and hard. First, teams must play 80-odd regular season games and win enough times to get into the playoffs. Then they must survive a two-month long battle of several win-or-go-home series. And when the last two teams face off in the final, the battle intensifies. Only one of them can walk away with the Cup. Check out some of the gutsiest and grittiest ways the Cup was won.

The Goalie Gamble

Coach Dick Irvin had a huge problem. His team, the Montreal Canadiens, was just one game away from elimination in the 1953 Stanley Cup playoffs. What's more, goalie Gerry McNeil had cracked under the pressure of losing the last three games. McNeil was begging Irvin to replace him. What was Irvin to do? Should he roll the dice and pull the veteran out of the net and stick in the rookie Jacques Plante, who had little playoff experience? Irvin said nothing. He called a practice the morning of the game. McNeil fanned on tons of shots and Plante was all over the puck. After practice, McNeil made another private plea to Irvin to pull him. But it wasn't until Irvin ran into Plante on the way to the rink for the game that he said, "You're in goal tonight, Jacques, and you are going to get us a shutout." Plante was stunned. So were the rest of the team. To calm the players' nerves, Irvin took another gamble. He held up some money and offered to bet every player a dollar that Plante would get a shutout. Irvin knew that no one would bet, because that would mean betting against the team. Instead, the players banded together to play really well. Irvin's gamble paid off. The Canadiens won the game, Plante got a shutout, and the team went on to win the Cup.

SCIENCE AT Play

Anything for Stanley

Teams will do anything to win the Stanley Cup. In 1905, Rat Portage challenged Ottawa for the Cup. The Rat Portage players laced up in thin-bladed tube skates, and zoomed circles around the sluggish Ottawa players to win the first game. But when they showed up for the second game in Ottawa, the rink looked like a swimming pool. It had been flooded with a few inches of water. The wet surface cancelled out Rat Portage's superior speed and puck-handling skills, while Ottawa lumbered through the slush to tie the series and win the next game.

THE ROAD TO STANLEY
REGULAR   82   games
PLAYOFFS   16-28 games

MANY SECTIONS OF THE ROAD
ARE BUMPY & HARD TO GET BY.
THERE ARE NO SHORT CUTS
AND THERE ARE NO DETOURS.
MAY THE BEST TEAM WIN!

Brett Hull Scores No Goal

When Brett Hull retired in 2005, he was the third top NHL scorer of all time. Nevertheless, throughout his career, Hull said he woke up every day "scared to death" that he might never score another goal. In 1999, the Dallas Stars acquired Hull, hoping he would be the extra firepower they needed to win the Cup. "Do you know how much pressure that is?" Hull once said. The Stars fought their way to the final round of the playoffs. Early in the final series against the Buffalo Sabres, Hull's knee was injured in a hit. Hull felt more pressure as he played through the rest of the series hurt. With Dallas leading the series 3 games to 2 and the score tied 1 — 1 in triple overtime, Hull limped to the front of the net and shot. The puck rebounded off goalie Dominik Hasek back to Hull and then Hull jammed it past Hasek for the Cup-winning goal. The Stars leapt off the bench and mobbed Hull in a victorious group hug. The only problem was that television replays showed Hull's skate in the goal crease before his stick brought the puck there. Back then, goals were disallowed if a player entered the crease before the puck. The Sabres and their fans protested, saying it was "no goal." And the officials? Well, the goal judge lit the lamp, so the goal stood. Nobody was more relieved than Hull.

The School of Grit

In 1983, the Edmonton Oilers—Wayne Gretzky, Mark Messier, Kevin Lowe, and company—were flying high. They were young, they were fast, and they liked to bury opponents in a mountain of goals. They had placed third overall in the NHL and blitzed their way into the Stanley Cup final, where they met the reigning champs, the New York Islanders. That's when the Oilers fell back to Earth. The Islanders' goalie Billy Smith shut them out in the first game. The Islanders outscored them 6 — 3 in the second game, and swept them out of the competition in four games straight. The Oilers felt completely dejected. As they filed out after the game, they dreaded passing by the Islanders' locker room and seeing the winners having a ball and drinking champagne from the Cup. But that wasn't the scene at all. The Islanders were groaning, icing injuries, and stitching up cuts. The Oilers were dumbfounded. They had lost the Cup and the Islanders had won, because the Islanders had given everything they had. "That's how you win championships," Lowe said to Gretzky. It was a lesson the Oilers took to heart as they won the Stanley Cup the next five out of seven seasons.

"I can't hear him. My two Stanley Cup rings are clogging up my ears."
— Patrick Roy during the 1996 playoffs when Jeremy Roenick questioned whether he was still a big-game goaltender

THEY SAID It!

THE GAME WAS NEVER THE SAME

Many people insist that Dallas stole the Cup in 1999 with Brett Hull's controversial goal (see above). NHL officials said that a puck that rebounds off a goalie doesn't change possession when picked back up by the shooter. So Hull, the shooter, still had possession and control of the puck and, therefore, could shoot and score a goal with his foot in the crease. Sound wishy-washy? The NHL got a lot of flak for defending the goal. And the very next season, the league dropped the rule that disallowed a goal if the player entered the goal crease before the puck.

STRANGE BUT TRUE

Bill Barilko Ignites the Leafs

The final series in the 1951 battle for the Stanley Cup was as close and thrilling as they come. Arch rivals the Toronto Maple Leafs and the Montreal Canadiens held nothing back. They played all five games down to the wire, requiring sudden-death overtime to decide each and every one.

Bashin' Bill Barilko was in fine form. The strapping young Leaf defender, known for his big heart and sunny smile, had been playing with unmatched exuberance throughout the playoffs. Barilko threw bone-crushing body checks, dropped to his knees to block shots, and even potted a few goals.

Heading into OT in game five, the Leafs were one goal away from winning the Cup. Coach Joe Primeau didn't want any rash moves from Barilko, who often bedeviled him by cutting loose on dazzling rushes. So he made Barilko promise not to desert his position on the blue line by going into the Canadiens' end.

Early in OT, a couple of Leaf forwards stormed over the Canadiens' blue line. But they didn't manage to connect for a goal. The puck hit a skate and slid to the face-off circle. Well, that loose puck was too much for Barilko to pass up. The big defender bombed in from the blue line and tripped over a teammate's skate to bash the puck. Barilko flew through the air and his shot flew into the net. The red light went on behind the goalie and Leaf fans exploded, whooping up a roar louder than any heard in the Gardens before.

Coach Primeau bounded over the boards and gave the cocky defender a big hug. Barilko's goal won the Cup and made him a hero. But he didn't have much time to savor the victory.

That summer, Barilko flew to James Bay to go fishing with a friend. And he never returned. Their plane got into trouble and Barilko vanished without a trace. His body didn't turn up until 1962. The strange thing was that the Leafs didn't win another Cup till then either. They fell short the whole time Barilko was "missing in action."

CHAPTER SEVEN

SO YOU
WANT TO BE A HOCKEY PLAYER

Do you dream of playing in the big leagues one day? It's not easy to get into professional hockey. Every year, the NHL holds an entry draft, where each team picks players from junior hockey. But that doesn't mean these players have made it. Some don't make it through training camp or crack the regular lineup. They get sent back to the minors and only play with the team if a regular player gets injured. Others make the team and then struggle to adjust to the caliber of NHL play. Some take years to reach their potential. Experts say that it takes size, strength, and speed to succeed in professional hockey. It also takes grit, heart, determination, and hard work. You must skate well, pass well, see the ice well—and you must believe in yourself no matter what. Despite all this, some rookies begin to shine as soon as they enter the NHL. Meet some of hockey's brightest stars, find out how one idol can inspire another, and get the scoop on just what it means to make it in the pros.

SKATE FAST AND CARRY THE PUCK

THE CHAIN OF IDOLS

What would you do if your favorite hockey player gave you his or her stick? Would you fall over? Would you jump for joy? Would it inspire you to aim high? Check out some of the amazing effects that a "brush with an idol" has had on some of the game's greatest players.

9
MR. HOCKEY

When the Great One, a.k.a. Wayne Gretzky, was 10 years old, he dreamed of playing just like Gordie Howe. Howe was a tough right-winger with a strong, quick shot who broke almost every scoring record in the NHL book. Imagine young Gretzky's delight when he met his idol at a special dinner. Howe gave the young player a piece of advice: "Work on your backhand." Gretzky took it to heart. He developed a strong backhand, which made him an even greater scoring threat.

87
THE NEXT ONE

When Sidney Crosby was 14, he played a game with his idol Wayne Gretzky. "He saw the game the same way I did when I was 14," said Gretzky. Later, when a reporter asked Gretzky if anyone could beat his scoring records, he said "Sidney Crosby. He's dynamite." And no one was more surprised than Crosby: "I will be the first one to say that I will not break his records. But for him to say that I could means I'm doing something right." And so maybe Crosby really is "the Next One."

99
THE GREAT ONE

When Wayne Gretzky played junior hockey, he wanted to wear Gordie Howe's number. But another player already had the number 9, so Gretzky went with 99 instead and never looked back. When he entered the big leagues, Gretzky began breaking Howe's scoring records, completely rewriting the record book as he romped through the NHL on a scoring tear that lasted throughout his career. And the two record-breaking juggernauts fast became friends.

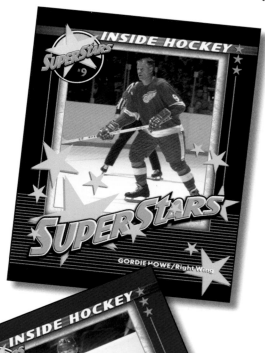

"Don't change."
— Gordie Howe's playing advice to a kid named Sidney Crosby

THEY SAID It!

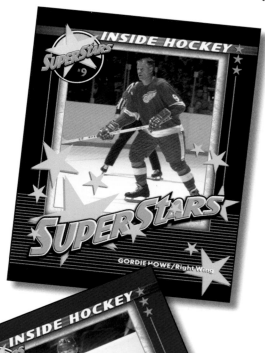INSIDE HOCKEY SuperStars — GORDIE HOWE/Right Wing

WAYNE GRETZKY/Center

SIDNEY CROSBY/Center

KEN DRYDEN / Goalie

PATRICK ROY / Goalie

MARTIN BRODEUR /

33
SAINT PATRICK

In 1985, Patrick Roy's wish came true: the rookie goalie got to play goal for his boyhood heroes, the Montreal Canadiens. In fact, the Habs named the rookie as their starting goaltender. Roy quickly gave Montreal fans lots to cheer about as he shut out most of his opponents' firepower like a brick wall. The young goalie was a fierce competitor who played to win. His miraculous performance between the pipes that year led the Canadiens all the way to Stanley Cup victory—and fans to call him St. Patrick. What's more, Roy won the Conn Smythe trophy as the MVP of the playoffs just like his idol Ken Dryden had in his rookie season.

29
THE THIEVING GIRAFFE

Seven-year-old Patrick Roy loved playing street hockey. He was the smallest kid in the 'hood, so he always played goal. Roy liked to imagine he was Ken Dryden, the 1.93 m (6 ft. 4 in.) goalie, in net for the Montreal Canadiens. In 1971, the Canadiens called up Dryden from their farm team and he helped them win six games straight. Then the Habs took a chance and left the rookie between the pipes for the playoffs. Dryden was awesome. The tall goalie was soon called the Thieving Giraffe for his remarkable ability to rob shooters of seemingly sure goals. Dryden backstopped the Canadiens all the way to Stanley Cup victory and won the Conn Smythe trophy as the Most Valuable Player.

30 MARTY

Kid goalie Martin Brodeur was watching closely when Patrick Roy became the youngest player to win the playoff's MVP award. Brodeur's dad was the Hab's official photographer, so Marty had a rink-side view for games. He studied Roy's infamous style of dropping to his knees and fanning out his shins like the wings of a butterfly to create a wall in front of the net. Young Marty began incorporating some of Roy's moves into his own netminding. Seeing such a young goalie play so successfully made Marty think that he might be able to play that well himself. And in his second NHL season, Brodeur did just that. He tended net to help the New Jersey Devils win the Stanley Cup.

Inside Scoop: Ken Dryden wasn't the only goalie Patrick Roy looked up to as a kid. Roy also idolized Dan Bouchard. One time, Roy even met Bouchard in person. Bouchard gave the kid his stick and Roy was over the moon. He slept with Bouchard's stick every night and dreamed of becoming a pro goalie one day.

LEGENDS ON ICE

SID THE KID VS.

Sidney Crosby and Alexander Ovechkin

They were rivals even before they got to the NHL. In 2003, Sidney Crosby watched from the sidelines as Alexander Ovechkin and the young Russian machine outgunned Team Canada to win the 2003 World Junior Championship. Crosby, too young to play for the team at 15 years old, had the honor of being the team's stick boy at training camp and gaining an insider's view of the action.

Two years later, at the 2005 World Junior Championship, Crosby got a chance to go head to head with Ovechkin himself. How would the wonder kid from Cole Harbour, Nova Scotia, stack up against the Russian phenom hailed as the top 19-year-old player in the world? The match-up between the two rising stars was the talk of the tournament.

It came in the final and deciding game. All the hype didn't seem to faze either of them one bit. "I've never seen him play," said Ovechkin of Crosby. "I think he's a good player. But I don't play against Crosby. I play against Team Canada. Hockey is a team game." And Crosby said, "We [the Canadians] came here to win gold."

Team Canada's Coach Brent Sutter matched Crosby's line with Ovechkin's line shift for shift. Early in the first period, Canada pounced on the puck for two unanswered goals. Then Ovechkin carried the puck to the Canadian blue line and cut to the middle of the ice.

SCIENCE AT Play

Rock-Solid Balance

Ever notice how hard it is to knock Sidney Crosby off the puck? When he was 14 years old, he began a unique training program to build balance and flexibility, improve his skating stride, and make his skating muscles more efficient. His personal trainer tried to knock him off his feet during workouts and create awkward circumstances for him to work through. The result? Crosby became stronger and learned how to keep his balance when players try to throw him off in games. He can receive, carry, and dish off the puck at lightning speeds and even score when he's on his knees!

ALEXANDER THE GREAT

Crosby saw Ovechkin but Ovechkin didn't see him. Crosby zoomed toward Ovechkin and thrust his hip and shoulder into the big Russian forward. Wham, bam! Ovechkin went down with a thud. The open-ice hit seemed to daze him. But he got up and skated away on his own steam. However after a few more shifts, he left the game. Crosby's hit took Ovechkin out of the action and gave the young Russian a separated shoulder. Canada then trounced the Russians, 6 – 1, for the gold medal.

But the rivalry between Sid the Kid and Alexander the Great was far from over. In 2004, Ovechkin became the top draft pick of the NHL. A year later, Crosby was the top pick. But since the NHL players were locked out for the entire 2004–2005 season, they both entered the NHL as rookies in 2005. Many people said Crosby was a shoo-in for Rookie of the Year. But Ovechkin's deft scoring touch and bone-rattling body checks soon endeared him to fans and hockey journalists. Many people said Ovechkin was the most exciting young player to watch on the ice. And the race for Rookie of the Year was on.

Partway through the season, Ovechkin pulled ahead of Crosby in the points department. Despite a strong point drive to finish the season, Crosby never quite caught up. Ovechkin finished with 106 points and Crosby 102. What's more, Ovechkin became only the second rookie in history to score 50 goals and rack up more than 100 points. He won Rookie of the Year. And the rivalry between the two young guns continues to fire up the league every time they meet.

"For me and him, it's a healthy competition."
—Sidney Crosby on his rivalry with Alexander Ovechkin

THEY SAID It!

Inside Scoop: Even though Alexander Ovechkin grew up in Russia, his idol was Wayne Gretzky. Ovechkin's dad got copies of the Great One's best games. They watched the tapes together and tried to figure out Gretzky's every move!

MAKING It

Making it in the NHL is a funny business. Where else would a player be expected to play hockey like the greatest basketball player? Or not measure up even though he scored a pile of goals? Or feel incomplete without the Stanley Cup?

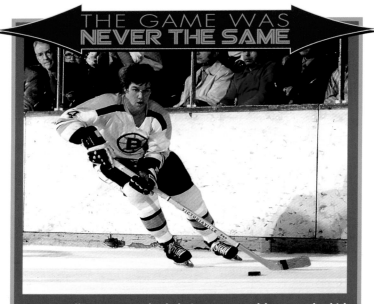

THE GAME WAS NEVER THE SAME

In 1962, all NHL scouts had their eye on Bobby Orr. The kid defender was about to turn 14 and none of them wanted him to get away. In those days, teams could sign a player for life at the tender age of 14. Orr was a young defender like they had never seen before. When he was on the ice, Orr completely controlled the game. He carried the puck deep into the attacking zone, skated circles around opponents, and feathered perfect passes onto teammates' sticks. And, boy, could he score! After deliberating for months, Orr signed with the Boston Bruins. He went on to win the NHL scoring championship not once but twice—a truly remarkable feat in an era when defenders didn't usually venture far into their opponent's territory. And it wasn't long before the radical way Orr played changed the role of defenders in the game.

Small Guy = Big Things

"You're too small to play, dude." If Martin St. Louis had listened to everyone who told him that, he might never have played hockey. Doubts about his height have dogged him since he was a kid. When St. Louis went to play major junior hockey, the league said he wasn't tall enough to play yet. So he joined a neighborhood team instead. When the 1.75 m (5 ft. 9 in.) forward finished college, he did not get drafted. Every single NHL team passed on him. Not one of them cared that he had set several scoring records during four seasons at the University of Vermont. And they didn't see that his size and speed actually help him zip past opposing checkers. Later, the Calgary Flames signed him as a free agent. But they didn't seem to believe in him much as they didn't give him much ice time. Nevertheless, St. Louis always believed in himself and refused to give up his dream of playing pro hockey. When the Tampa Bay Lightning signed him in 2000, they believed in him, too. Finally, St. Louis got the chance to prove all the doubters wrong. In 2004, he won the NHL scoring race, helped Tampa Bay win the Stanley Cup, and won the MVP award of the year. And do you know what the five-foot-nine scoring demon said on award night? He confessed that he is actually one inch shorter!

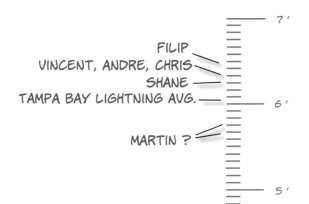

7'

FILIP

VINCENT, ANDRE, CHRIS

SHANE

TAMPA BAY LIGHTNING AVG.

6'

MARTIN ?

5'

Mission 16W

Ray Bourque had it all. As soon as the crack defender skated into the NHL, a stack of awards piled up at his feet. He won the Rookie of the Year award. He made it onto the all-star teams 17 times and walked off with the Best Defenseman award five times. But he felt something was missing. In all his 20 years with the Boston Bruins, Bourque had never won the Stanley Cup. The Bruins had reached the finals twice and lost both times. Some people say that winning the Cup is the mark of a true champion, and that those who have never won it just don't measure up. So partway through his 21st season, Bourque asked to be traded to a Cup contender. He went to the Colorado Avalanche and within 15 months he was a man on a mission. The Avalanche were in the playoff final and Bourque was wearing a cap emblazoned with "Mission 16W"— the magic number of wins for the Stanley Cup. But the New Jersey Devils took the lead in the series, 3 games to 2, and it looked like the Stanley Cup might slip away again. Before Game 6, Bourque gave a stirring speech in the dressing room, saying that everything in his career came down to the game tonight. The Avalanche went all out and won the game and then won Game 7 to clinch the Cup. When Captain Steve Yzerman accepted the trophy, he gave it to Bourque immediately. Bourque hoisted the Stanley Cup over his head in celebration as tears of joy ran down his face. He had helped his team capture the Cup. Mission accomplished.

The Curse of Michael Jordan

In 1998 the Tampa Bay Lightning chose sharpshooter Vincent Lecavalier as the first pick overall in the NHL entry draft. Lightning owner Art Williams called the young hotshot the "Michael Jordan of hockey." Talk about pressure! Lecavalier laughed off the comparison to basketball's living legend, but his NHL career got off to a rocky start. At first, the 18-year-old got pushed around in the corners, having to learn how to hold his own against older players, some 23 kg (50 lbs.) heavier than him. What made things even tougher was that the Lightning were the last place team, and Lecavalier was expected to lift their fortunes. He became the youngest player at the time to be made captain. But coach John Tortorella didn't think Lecavalier was working hard enough. He called Lecavalier "Lazy Vinny," and stripped him of the captaincy. Lecavalier had his worst season ever. But next season he came to training camp in the best shape of his life. Lecavalier busted out offensively and racked up 78 points, more than any season before. The next year he helped the Lightning win the Stanley Cup and Team Canada the World Cup. Lecavalier was named World Cup MVP. And in 2007, he won the NHL scoring race. Finally, Lecavalier had shaken the curse and was on top again.

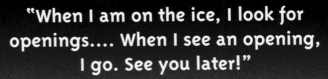

"When I am on the ice, I look for openings.... When I see an opening, I go. See you later!"

—Bobby Orr on how he played the game in the moment

THEY SAID It!

STRANGE BUT TRUE

One of the Guys

Hayley Wickenheiser was determined to be "one of the guys." In 2003, after she had helped Team Canada win gold at the 2002 Olympics, the star center was itching for a new challenge to take her game to the next level.

So she decided to hop on the ice with men. Sound crazy? Well, the girl from Shaunavon, Saskatchewan, had been doing that since she was five years old. "I always used to play with the boys, since we didn't have a girls' team where I came from," Wickenheiser told the press.

Back then, Wickenheiser was the only girl on the team. She was so good and scored so many goals that she won the MVP award several times. Opponents slashed and checked her with a vengeance. They weren't going to let a girl be the best player in a boy's league if they could help it. Eventually, Wickenheiser cracked the women's Team Canada lineup. The Philadelphia Flyers were so impressed with her playing that they invited her to workout with the guys at a couple of training camps.

But neither the Flyers nor Wickenheiser ever considered the idea of her joining the team. Bodychecking is a huge part of the men's game in the NHL, where players hit each other against the boards or on the open ice. Bam! Wham! Slam! At 1.75 m (5 ft. 9 in.) and 76.5 kg (170 lbs), Wickenheiser just isn't big enough to dish it out like that.

So she headed to Europe, where the men's game focuses on passing and skating and the average player is more her size. Wickenheiser got a tryout with HC Salamat, a men's pro team in Finland, and won a spot on the team. The Finnish fans went bonkers, packing the rink each game to see her and chanting her name "Heli, Heli, Heli."

Wickenheiser insisted on no preferential treatment. She didn't avoid contact in games but she was careful. She became the first woman to score a goal in a men's pro game and won a remarkable 70 to 80 percent of faceoffs.

And the strange thing was that she really did seem to be one of the guys. Fans and journalists had a tough time spotting her on the ice. Once she was in uniform and a helmet, Wickenheiser blended right in. The only thing that gave her away was her skates. They were noticeably smaller than the guys'. In fact, some fans even looked for her by looking for small skates!

THEM'S FIGHTING MOVES

CHAPTER EIGHT

All it takes is a couple of shoves. Two opponents chase the puck into a corner. They push and shove each other against the boards, jamming sticks and skates as they battle for the puck. Then the next thing you know, they drop their sticks and gloves and their fists fly, delivering deliberate blows as each player tries to pummel the other into a pulp. What is it about playing hockey that brings out people's fighting spirit? Maybe it's getting a stick in the face, or getting flattened against the boards, or getting an elbow in the mouth. The fact is, fighting and hitting have been part of the game since the beginning, and some hockey experts believe they are integral to winning. Take a walk on the tough side and get the scoop on what makes some of the toughest teams and players tick.

GET READY TO
RUMBLE!

ROCK 'EM SOCK 'EM

Some players will brawl until they sprawl or crawl. Check out some of the toughest guys, biggest hits, and strangest forces that have ever rocked and socked the game.

She Shoots! She Scores! She Hits!

In the 1930s, the Preston Rivulettes (above) ruled the ice like no other team in the history of hockey. Of the 350 games the Rivs played, they lost only two. Sisters Hilda and Nellie Ranscombe, Marm and Helen Schmuck, Myrtle Parr, and teammates played by men's rules, and they could skate, stickhandle, and swing their fists like the best of them. Other teams got so frustrated always losing to the Rivs, they became hostile. "Sticks and fists fly freely," screamed newspaper headlines, as fights broke out on and off the ice. One time, a Port Dover opponent knocked down star forward Hilda Ranscombe and socked her like a punching bag until the referee pulled her off. Another time, an angry mob of Port Dover fans ran at the Rivs for beating their team, and the players had to hightail it out of town with a police escort. And when a referee admitted to a biased call that cost the Rivs a game, one of the Schmuck sisters jumped him and let him have it until teammates pulled her off. Talk about not losing without a fight!

When Brute Force Fails...

In the 1920s, Howie Morenz, a.k.a. the Stratford Streak, was the hardest player to stop. "Howie comes at you with such speed that it's almost impossible to block him with a body check," opponent Eddie Shore once said. One time, when Shore and fellow defender Lionel Hitchman went to sandwich Morenz between their two hulking bodies, Morenz shot forward eluding their grasp just like a slippery bar of soap popping out of a pair of hands. And even when bruisers like Shore managed to nail Morenz against the boards, they couldn't knock Morenz off his game. Morenz would just rush down the ice and storm the net with his deadly shot again and again. If anything, the more hits he took, the harder he played. Knowing that brute force couldn't stop him, one team tried a different force altogether—the police. No joke! The Preston team had a police officer charge Morenz for "malicious damage to property," citing that he had slashed the rubbers of the goal judge as he skated around the net.

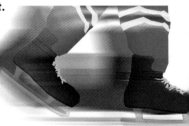

The officer was about to drag Morenz off to court. But once Stratford fans got wind of the charge, they offered to pay for a new pair of rubbers and the charge was dropped.

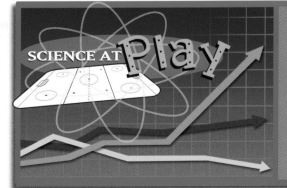

SCIENCE AT Play

Three Men in the Box

Statistics show there's a huge increase in scoring when three players are off the ice in the penalty box. In the 1970s, Roger Neilson, coach of the Toronto Maple Leafs, devised a scheme to take advantage of this. When the Leafs were on the power play with a one-player advantage, he sent Tiger Williams out on the ice. Williams' job was to provoke an opponent into taking a swing at him and then swing back, so the ref would send them both to the penalty box. Against Vancouver, this tactic resulted in several goals. But once the NHL wised up to the scam, they outlawed it. They made a rule that said the offenders would have to serve penalties, but the number of players on the ice would remain unchanged.

A Tiger On Ice

Facing off against the Broad Street Bullies (see page 60) never got to Dave "Tiger" Williams the way it did to many players. "I went out wanting everybody to pick a fight with me," Tiger once said. "I was so pumped up I didn't care if I was hit." One time, when Broad Street Bully Dave "The Hammer" Schultz went to nail him with a punch, Williams bit the Hammer on the nose! When Williams was just five years old, his first coach called him Tiger for his tenacious play and "go get 'em" spirit. The little tyke couldn't skate that well but that didn't stop him from pouncing on every opportunity to get into the action. And that trait stayed with Williams throughout his entire on-ice career. In Toronto, Williams went after any player who jostled the Leafs' top guns Darryl Sittler and Lanny McDonald. One time he even whacked opposing coach Scotty Bowman over the head with his stick. The incident earned Tiger a one game suspension. But Tiger wasn't a complete "animal" on the ice. He could also score. You might say Tiger gave opponents a lot to growl about!

The Hit Man

Scott Stevens had a reputation for taking out opponents with bone-crushing hits. "When he's out on the ice, you feel his presence," teammate Scott Gomez once said. The 1.88 m (6 ft. 2 in.) defender could fire up his team with a single glare or bodyslamming open-ice check. And when the hit man's punishing shoulder caught opponents unaware, it often snuffed their "lights out." During the 2000 playoffs, Stevens threw what some people say is the greatest open-ice hit of all time. Eric "the Big E" Lindros skated over the defender's blue line with the puck. His head was down and he didn't see Stevens coming. Bam! The hit was vintage Stevens: clean, violent, and completely devastating. Stevens' shoulder plowed into Lindros' jaw and knocked the Big E out cold. Lindros crumpled to the ice and when he came to he had a wicked concussion that kept him out of the game, the rest of the playoffs, and a good chunk of the next season. In fact, some say Lindros was never the same player afterward. TV stations played replays of the monster hit over and over. And though the hit man felt bad about sidelining Lindros, he wasn't about to change his style. "Hitting is part of the game," said Stevens. "That's the bottom line. I get hit and I'm going to give a hit." Spoken like a true hit man, or what?

"I hated it. But it's playoff time and playoff time is war."

— New Jersey Devils' defender Scott Stevens on the publicity that swirled around his brutal open-ice hit on Eric Lindros

THEY SAID It!

THE BROAD STREET BULLIES

The Philadelphia Flyers of the 1970s

No team left Broad Street, home of the Philadelphia Flyers, without fresh cuts and bruises in the 1970s. In fact, just the thought of meeting the Flyers—a.k.a. The Broad Street Bullies or the Mean Machine—on their home turf did some players in. No kidding! Players often came down with a sudden bout of "Philadelphia flu" that caused them to sit out the entire game.

The Broad Street Bullies were a lineup of tough characters: Bobby "The Clobber" Clarke, Dave "The Hammer" Schultz," Bill "The Cowboy" Flett, Bob "Hound" Kelly, Don "Big Bird" Saleski, and André "Moose" Dupont. The whole team was eager to crush the competition. "We're a big club and hitting is a big part of our game," Coach Fred Shero once said. If an opponent scrapped with one of them, the rest of them would come looking for blood like a pack of wolves.

Even when they weren't cruising for a bruising, the Broad Street Bullies were nasty. Coach Shero's playing orders were to "arrive first to the puck and in ill humor." And that's exactly what the Bullies did. They ran over opponents who came between them and the puck, creamed opponents into the boards, and flew at opponents with bashing elbows, racking up more penalty minutes than any NHL team before.

But the Flyers didn't win games by bully tactics alone. They also used sheer hard work. The leader of the pack was captain Bobby Clarke. "Clarke is our leader," goalie Bernie Parent once said.

Inside Scoop: One season, The Hammer, Big Bird, Hound, and Moose ran completely roughshod, getting 200 or more penalty minutes each. And with that the infamous "200 Club" was born.

"The leader of the pack was captain Bobby Clarke."

"He works so hard himself that the other guys just have to work to keep up. He is the guy who makes us go."

Besides being a hard worker, Clarke was also a gifted scorer and playmaker who fed the puck to teammates for scoring chances. But what made Clarke truly remarkable was his ability to dig deeper than anyone thought was humanly possible and compel his teammates to victory.

The Flyers soon became the most popular team in the league. Still, many said they were nothing but a goon squad who injected unnecessary violence into the game. However, these critics often overlooked the incredible teamwork that made the Mean Machine click and tick. Each Flyer had a role to play and the team valued all their contributions equally. This teamwork combined with toughness and hard work led the Broad Street Bullies to two Stanley Cup victories back to back and kept them hovering at the top of the NHL pack for several seasons.

"I'd rather fight than score."
— Dave "The Hammer" Schultz

THEY SAID It!

THE GAME WAS NEVER THE SAME

In the old days, superstars like Gordie Howe and Rocket Richard swung their fists to fight their own battles. That began to change around 1960, when the enforcer hit the ice. As an enforcer, a player's job was to police the ice to protect star players and fight for the team. Some say the first enforcer was John Ferguson (see left). Others say it was Reginald Fleming. Both Fleming and Ferguson could score as well as fight. But their role as tough guys, who wielded muscle and brawn, eventually paved the way for players whose only job was to beat up the opposition, like Dave Schultz (right). In the 1970s, the Flyers seemed to turn the enforcer role upside-down by playing with the motto: If you fight one of us, you fight the whole team.

John Ferguson

Dave "The Hammer" Schultz

STRANGE BUT TRUE

The Edmonton Express Roars Up the Ice

Look out! Here comes the Edmonton Express! In the 1920s and 1930s, Eddie Shore was like a runaway freight train. Every time the aggressive defender rushed down the ice, he got everyone's attention. "He would either end up bashing somebody, get into a fight, or score a goal," Hammy Moore, trainer of the Boston Bruins, said.

Back then, most players threw body checks awkwardly, often lifting their sticks or drawing a penalty. But not Shore. He could hit an opposing sniper with his body—ka-pow!—and carry right on playing. Shore played through injury after injury. And in doing so, he set the "play till you drop" warrior code that NHL players follow today.

When the rugged defender joined the Boston Bruins, Boston fans took to calling him "Old Blood and Guts." The Bruins played up this image for all it was worth. They had Shore enter the rink wearing a bullfighter's cape to the tune of "Hail to the Chief." A valet would remove the cape so that Shore could rip up the ice unencumbered.

And in a 1929 game against the Montreal Maroons, Shore did just that. He put up his dukes not one but five times, setting a record for the most fights in a game. By the time the last punch was thrown, Shore looked like a human train wreck. He had a broken nose, four missing teeth, two black eyes, cuts over both eyes, a gash on his cheek, and a concussion. An ambulance carted him off along with two Maroons he had traded blows with.

When Shore hung up his skates, he began coaching with his iron fist. To stop goalie Don Simmons from falling to the ice, Shore tied the goalie's arms to the crossbar of the net and had the team fire shots on Simmons. And the strange thing was that Old Blood and Guts made the entire team take ballet and tap dancing. When they were on the road, he even made them practice the dance steps in hotel lobbies. Shore believed dance improved balance and that balance was the base of athletic ability. The fact is, if you've got good balance, you're less likely to be knocked off your feet by a blow to the head!

PHOTO CREDITS

INDEX